AISHA MY SISTER

Aisha My Sister

A Handbook for Christians Relating to
Muslim Women

Sally Sutcliffe

solway

Copyright @ Sally Sutcliffe 1997

First published in the UK 1997 by Solway

03 02 01 00 99 98 97   7 6 5 4 3 2 1

Solway is an imprint of Paternoster Publishing,
P.O. Box 300, Carlisle, Cumbria CA3 0QS UK

British Library Cataloguing in Publication Data

A catalogue record for this book is available from the British Library.

ISBN 1-900507-44-7

Typeset by WestKey Ltd, Falmouth, Cornwall
Printed in the UK by Mackays of Chatham PLC, Kent.

CONTENTS

Foreword

The gospel is the most precious news for humankind, and Muslim females are the most unreached group of people on this planet. Many Muslim women I have known have felt disadvantaged within Islam. The heart of the Christian gospel is that there is justice for everybody; this is wonderful news for Muslim women. It is the burning desire of my heart that Muslim women the world over will hear the good news about the God who chose to send Christ into this world through a woman.

Seventeen years working in inner London have shown me that the hustle and bustle of city life puts many strains and pressures on Muslim women and their families. I firmly believe that the church has an important role to play in trying to alleviate these pressures. I feel that the most important thing for us all to learn is to listen and not to preach. We need to establish trust first. When Jesus spoke to people he started with ordinary, everyday things and events such as, 'Give me a drink of water' and 'Have you been married?' Eventually he led the woman at the well on to believe that he was the Messiah. Muslim women are not looking for charity or pity, but for friendship and dignified help, for a degree of spiritual fellowship and for a support system that back home the family would have provided.

We should ask ourselves, has the gospel made such an impact on my life that I am a living example to follow? The best way to witness to Muslim women is by example. We should not challenge them publicly about their views; we must respect them, otherwise our relationship will be destroyed straight away. Aggressive evangelism does more harm than good; it undermines their own belief system, background and identity. We must never forget that many Muslim women are very intelligent, well educated and gracious in their living even though they may be in reduced or deprived circumstances here in Britain. They are very loyal to their families and there are many good qualities we can learn from them. If we want to make an impact on the lives of Muslim women we must affirm the positive aspects of their lifestyle, and we must ensure that our own lifestyles at least match their standards. We need to spend years patiently befriending, accepting and loving them uncondi-tionally. Love and friendship shown over a period of years will eventually bear fruit.

Love cannot be preached; it must be shown in practice. As Christian women we can baby-sit for our Muslim friends and neighbours, invite them to go on holiday with us, accept them as adopted family members and in natural ways speak of our faith. Most Muslim women love to invite guests into their home and this is a wonderful way to begin to build friendships. We can offer help and in return we need to be prepared to receive help ourselves. All God-fearing families in Britain face similar tensions, problems and difficulties (such as raising children in today's secular society) and we must not be afraid to confess these to each other and support each other.

When Muslims decide to follow Jesus, we need to help them continue to love their families and communities; we should help them not to reject and condemn everything in their previous way of life since not everything they have come from is bad. Even with my own family, who are all Muslims, I have been able to keep the doors of communication open. May this book help you understand and love Muslim women in Britain and, as you live out your faith in Christ, may he bring them hope.

Bassi Mirzania

Bassi Mirzania arrived in this country from Iran in 1979. She was brought up in a Muslim family, and at the age of twenty-two became head of Kurdistan's social affairs programme. After five years providing relief for thousands of Shi'ite Muslim refugees fleeing from Iraq, she moved back to Tehran to work on the Shah of Persia's social welfare programme. In 1973 she became a Christian. Five years later, Revolutionary Guards stormed the palace; the Royal Family were swept away, Bassi's passport and documents were burnt and she was forced into hiding. She finally escaped to Britain and soon became Senior Social and Community Worker in Willesden (Diocese of London), a Social Responsibility Team Leader and the Bishop's Adviser on community affairs and social responsibilities. Her work with Brent Deanery brought her into contact with Muslim women and girls from all parts of the Muslim world. Her vision was to take the churches out into the community through providing centres for the mentally ill, single parents and isolated refugees. This involved contact with 38 nationalities and Bassi built up an army of 180 volunteers from the churches (mostly women) to serve the community. Bassi is now Director of Social Responsibility for the Diocese of Guildford.

Preface

The Parable of the Good Muslim Neighbour

When an elderly English member of an inner-city church had a nasty fall in her street, it was her Pakistani neighbours who rushed to the rescue. Her friend, who had always complained of 'them taking over our country' surprised herself (and her listeners) by the glowing praise with which she found herself telling the story: 'They were so kind'. And what did the rescued lady say? 'My neighbour took me into her home, laid me down on the couch, called the doctor, and gave me a cup of tea that tasted just like nectar.'

The one certainty for anyone entering into relationship across cultural and religious divides is that they are in for some surprises. This collection of stories, thoughts, snapshots and experiences is offered as a taster to those who are willing to take risks in reaching out to Muslim women, to step onto unfamiliar territory and probably be (pleasantly) surprised.

One quarter of the world's population is Muslim. At least fifty per cent are women. Some live here. In spite of that, it is still true to say that, like the majority who live beyond these shores, most have never met a Christian believer. And many Christians have never met a Muslim. Multicultural Britain now yields plenty of scope for such interactions. It also provides opportunities to overcome historical stereotypes and misunderstandings. We meet Muslims in all walks of life; many professions too now require the acquisition of cross-cultural skills and an understanding of people with different world-views from mainstream, secular, Anglo-Saxon society. What is our response as Christians to these opportunities?

This book is intended for Christian women of all denominations and backgrounds: lay women, ordained women, theological students, women with Muslim neighbours, women with Muslim colleagues, health care professionals, teachers, social workers and women who for some reason feel the Lord is calling them to reach out to Muslims. Though the book is mainly addressed to an imaginary Christian woman, who is white and was brought up with little contact with people from other cultures, we hope that Christian women from other backgrounds will read it too, for you are key people in getting the message across to the churches.

Aisha My Sister is designed for use by church groups as well as individuals. There are pointers for discussion in most chapters, though there may not always be a right or wrong answer! The book does not offer an in-depth analysis of Islam nor of the theology of outreach. It does, however, raise implications for sharing our faith, and offers pointers and suggestions based on our own experience. Note too that we have consciously chosen to speak of relationships with Muslim women, rather than Hindu or Sikh women. There are many other excellent resources on related subjects. See the Appendix for a list of resources for further study, including those covering Hindus and Sikhs in Britain.

This book could not have been written without the important insights and contributions of over twenty women of various cultural backgrounds and denominations. All are Christians with experience in building up friendships with Muslim women. Some were brought up in the Muslim faith but have decided to follow Jesus. Some are British Asians, born and brought up in multicultural Britain. Some are full-time Christian workers in mission agencies or churches, others meet Muslims through secular employment (community workers, social workers, health workers). They live in different areas of Britain, some in inner cities, other in suburbia. Some have lived in or were brought up in Muslim countries.

British Asian women and Asian, Iranian and Arabic women have a vital key to unlocking many of the complexities of multicultural society and faith, and are a living demonstration to churches in Britain of the true diversity and richness of the body of Christ. The importance of their wisdom and experiences cannot be stressed highly enough (see Chs. 8 to 10 in particular). We acknowledge, however, that we have not covered all areas: none of the contributors is from Afro-Caribbean communities, though we are aware that many Afro-Caribbean churches have outreach projects to their Asian neighbours.

The title *Aisha My Sister* was inspired by Anne Cooper's book on Islam and Christian witness, *Ishmael My Brother* (see Bibliography). As Christians we share with Muslims a common spiritual heritage since Abraham was the father of both Isaac and Ishmael. The history of how Isaac and Ishmael divided into the Jewish and Arab (Muslim) nations, and how there was enmity between them can be read in Genesis and followed through the course of the Old Testament. Yet also throughout the Bible there are stories of God repairing the damage of division and enmity, culminating in the reconciling death of Christ on the cross. Muslims are our sisters and brothers in Abraham if not in Christ. Christ can break through centuries-old barriers between Muslims, Jews and Christians. Can we follow his example in showing love to Aisha our sister?

Why a book about outreach to Muslim women only, not men? Much has been written by Christian men about outreach to Muslims in general, but very little has been written by Christian women about outreach to Muslim women in particular. There are very separate issues when reaching out to Muslim women; their world is quite distinct from the world of Muslim (and Christian) men. Many women up and down the country are already involved in building bridges of friendship with female neighbours and colleagues; this book seeks to encourage that to develop.

We have tried to avoid generalisations, which never help. 'Muslim women' are no less a unified group to be lumped together and characterised than are 'young people' or 'Europeans'. Though 1991 Census figures are much lower, unofficial estimates (including those of Muslim organisations) are that one- and-a-half million Muslims live in Britain, of which roughly half are women. There are as many variations of Muslim womanhood as there are individuals. There are secular Muslim women, devout Muslim women (both young and old), there are revivalist missionary-minded young women. There are women who understand their faith and, understanding it, believe all the more fervently. There are women who, having investigated the faith for themselves, have rejected it, though not their culture. There are some who have rejected both. And there are many who, like most of us, are in the process of moving from one position to another on their journey towards self-understanding.

Some Muslim women are highly educated students and lecturers from all over the world, here in transit. Much of the book, however, is based on contact with the settled communities of traditional, uneducated women from villages in Pakistan or Bangladesh. These women live in Britain's inner cities, often in poor housing and suffering economic disadvantage. Their children, born and bred in Britain suffer unemployment disproportionately. Racism is still very much a factor in many families' lives and it affects women particularly acutely.

But is all doom and gloom? Are Muslim women oppressed by their men folk? Is Islam a cruel religion? What is it really like for young Muslims living between two cultures? Muslims are often in the news, be it the Rushdie affair, religious education issues or arranged marriage sagas.

We hope this book will counteract the sensationalism of the press and 'lift the veil' off the stereotype of the down-trodden, oppressed, unconfident Muslim female we vaguely see in our mind's eye. Neither do we wish to deny there are women who are in this situation. But no community or culture is stagnant, however it may appear from the outsider's point of view. Much has changed and is changing in many women's lives. Most changes happen on the inside, and may go unnoticed for years by those who do not see beyond a person's clothes and culture. What changes are needed in our own lives?

If you find this book raises important issues; if your mind is opened to the tremendous richness of human encounter which is possible, and the opportunities to learn from and contribute to the lives of Muslim women in this country; if you have a burden for Muslim women to experience the joy of the Lord as you have, then can you encourage others to become involved? Why not start a prayer and/or discussion group with this book as a resource? Together as a group you can go on to take risks and build friendships.

Sally Sutcliffe

Note: Though the stories in the book are based on real events or facts, in many cases personal details have been changed to protect identities.

Acknowledgements

I would like to register my profound thanks to the many women (and one or two men) up and down the country, who have contributed to the making of this book. From the start, this has been a joint effort, to use the title of Michele Guinness's book, a *Tapestry of Voices*. My job as compiler has been to collect the 'material' and sew it together.

Several of the key Asian or former Muslim contributors have to remain anonymous; special thanks go to them for sharing their stories and for giving vital insights. Thanks also to all other contributors for many sensitive insights: Fareedeh Drever, Catriona Forbes, Abigail Kingston, Yvonne Malstead, Margaret Masood, Patty McCulloch, Bassi Mirzania, Pratima Mistry, Shuguftah, Susan Pullen, Paula Smithers, Ann Steer, Valerie Pope. Ida Glaser and Elsie Maxwell provided invaluable contributions and support. I should also like to acknowledge Anne Cooper, whose book *Ishmael My Brother* inspired the choice of title and who encouraged me along the way.

Thanks go to Interserve, for permission to reproduce 'No place like home', first published in GO magazine, third quarter 1995 and to the Yorkshire Baptist Association for permission to reproduce, in shortened form, 'A Story of a Friendship' from their publication *Faith at the Boundaries*. The poem 'Chauvinist Creation', copyright Gordon Bailey, is quoted on page 156 by kind permission of the author.

Particular thanks to Jenny Taylor (Paternoster commissioning editor) for guiding me through the publication process. Thanks are due to friends and family who have helped me keep my head above water.

My husband, Will, deserves a dedication all to himself; for his encouragement, proof-reading, and patience.

Biblical references are taken from the New International Version, Hodder & Stoughton.

Qur'anic references are taken from *The Holy Qur'an: Text, Translation and Commentary*, (Abdullah Yusuf Ali), originally published by the Islamic Education Centre, Jeddah in 1934.

Part I

Meeting Muslim Women

[1]

Starting Points

According to one Asian Christian woman, there are three starting points to sharing the love of Christ with our Muslim neighbours: prayer, love and knowledge.

Prayer is the starting point. It is God's love that we share, not our own. If we lack love, we can ask for it in prayer. But if we don't add knowledge, we'll very soon get stuck.

What do we need to know?

Firstly, we need to know God for ourselves. We can't share his love if we don't know him! 'We will find out on the Last Day who is right—you Christians or we Muslims!' said Mr Ali, with whose family I had been friendly for years. The knowledge that our friends may be equally sure of their faith and want us to embrace Islam may be somewhat unsettling. We may go on the defensive, and we may find our faith deeply challenged. Yet we may also sense the deep truth that God is big enough to defend himself.

Most Muslim women, unless they are highly educated, have a faith which is more concerned with felt needs than a detailed understanding of orthodox Islam. It is on this level of personal, day-to-day living that we can naturally share our experience of God. On one particularly tiring day, when I was feeling 100 per cent below par and recovering from a nasty bout of 'flu, when I had, it seemed to me, little to say to my friend about anything, let alone God, she remarked: 'When you speak of God, it is as if you know him! How can that be?' A good question, waking me from despondency and stimulating me to keep in step with the Spirit, however weak I felt. Chapters 8, 10 and 11 deal with some of the theological issues of sharing our faith.

Next, we need to know ourselves. Self-knowledge is based on self-perception but can be informed by the perception of others. How do we perceive ourselves? 'In the West . . . we value the freedom of the individual, the right to self-expression, the primary importance of wealth-creation, efficiency, "love" and personal security.'[1] How does the Muslim community perceive us? Over the centuries, western women (regarded as 'Christian') have been seen to be immoral, wilful, disrespectful, immodest and self-interested. The West has also been seen as the home, not only of the lascivious film industry but of the colonialist who ruled Muslim societies to his own advantage. Now the West is also believed to be seeking to secularize Muslim youth, seeing Islam as a cultural and religious threat.

Whatever background we come from, we need to understand our own culture, so that we can recognize good and bad in it. We also need to distinguish which of our beliefs and actions are really Christian, and which are just part of our national and cultural heritage—there's a big difference. The Indian subcontinent is scattered with monuments to the gospel according to British culture (redbrick Victorian cathedrals with pews).

Many of us who have entered into relationships with Muslim women and families have probably at some point been shocked when we have recognized the unconscious assumptions we had made about our friends. It may take us a while to unlearn some myths we have grown up with. Jesus, we discover, was not white with blue eyes and fair hair as our Victorian forebears portrayed (and you can still find such Aryan paintings displayed in village churches in Pakistan), nor is Christianity a western religion.

Do we have any subtly condescending attitudes? What are our motives? Are we responding out of a need to be needed? Will we resist the temptation to become indispensable? And as one Muslim woman put it, 'Do you love me because you want me to follow Christ or do you want me to follow Christ because you love me?'

Finally, we need to know our neighbours. How do we perceive Muslims? Over the centuries, the 'Christian' West has regarded Muslims as barbaric, misogynistic, untrustworthy, unenlightened and a threat to Christendom. Muslim women have been regarded as a silent, almost faceless, oppressed group, with no powers over any part of their or their family's lives. Muslim men have been seen as cruel tyrants and religious hypocrites, leading selfish, debauched lives.

Are these jaundiced perceptions the reason why many Christians and Muslims are afraid of each other? The Bible has a lot to say about fear. Mostly, it says, 'Fear not!' 'There is no fear in love. But perfect love casts out fear . . .'[2]

Anyone who has travelled outside the boundaries of their own culture will find it easier to understand the situation for their Muslim friends in Britain. They will also find it easier to regard cultural differences as positives, rather than negatives. Once we start on the adventure of cross-cultural encounter, there are infinite possibilities for our under-standing of others, and ourselves, to be increased. We'll make many mistakes, as will our friends and we may be misinterpreted. But it will be worthwhile.

Many white British people say: 'When in Rome, do as the Romans do', in defence of the view that if Asians have come to live here, they should follow 'our ways'. There is some truth in this, though it is not such a simple equation. First, we may not appreciate that already, in coming to Britain, Muslim families have had to make many adjust-ments, and have tried to understand the society they entered. The way society is organized, the way houses and streets are built, the indoor, rather than the outdoor life, the emphasis on the individual, the lack of hospitality are all factors which have demanded adjustments in their way of life. Secondly, some may feel so insecure that they need to blot out any good they see in the outside community, for fear of losing their own identity. Others, in trying to be accepted, may adjust too much and reject their own culture entirely. Another factor is where Muslims live. If they live in decayed inner cities, they may see 'our ways' as mini-skirts, vandalism and moral decay; no wonder they do not want to follow them.

Perhaps the 'Brits abroad' can offer a model of how to adapt? Anyone who lived under the Raj knows that most colonialists not only pursued their own way of life, wearing English clothes, eating English food, importing ice cubes, speaking English among themselves, but they also regarded their culture as superior and tried to impose it. There were notable exceptions (such as Lawrence of Arabia), who were often accused of 'going native'. Nowadays, Brits abroad may not have the colonialistic powers of yesteryear, but no doubt they still, like all human beings, find cultural adjustment difficult. The natural response to cultural alienation is to retreat within the old familiar identity rather than actively to adopt the new.

Another point is that, as the host culture, and particularly if we are Christians, the onus is on us to make the approach towards our Muslim neighbours. As Christians we are free, as Paul was, to live both under and outside the law. He could be a Jew to the Jews or a Gentile to the Gentiles because of the freedom he had in Christ. Muslims do not have the same freedom to become a Christian to the Christians, for they, like the Jews, are under the law. As Paul says, we Christians have a duty not to take our freedom lightly, either by creating stumbling-blocks for those weaker in the faith (or outside the faith), or by assuming others should follow our ways when they themselves are not set free.[3]

Look through the Bible and see how often God's people needed to learn to open up to others across divides of culture, race and creed. Peter was surprised that the Lord had already been speaking to Cornelius before he (Peter) arrived. Many incidents in the Bible suggest that the outcast, foreigner and believer of a different creed and culture has much to teach the believer. Why was it that of the ten lepers who were healed, the only one to come back and say thank you was the foreigner?

Discuss

- *Study Romans 14 and 1 Corinthians 8 and 9. How does Paul's argument apply to Christians relating and witnessing cross-culturally to Muslims?*

Getting to know you

Our Muslim women friends are not usually worried if we put our proverbial foot in it to begin with. Anyway, who wants to make friends with a know-it-all? Muslims are just people like you and me. We are all the same under the skin; we experience most of the same joys, sorrows and the same needs for food, water, shelter, dignity as a person and love. But we do need to look and listen, so that we can understand how our Muslim neighbours think and feel about life. We can get to know our area, finding out whether Asian citizens are majority Muslim, Hindu or Sikh (or Christian) and how nominal or devout; whether communities are mainly first, second or third generation. Community centres and libraries have information on local faiths and major languages spoken. The 1991 Census County Monitors and Ward and Civil Parish Monitor Factsheets give a breakdown of various statistics, including ethnic groups. You can ask The Office for National Statistics for the one for your own area. Social surveys on ethnic minorities are also available. (See 'Other Organisations' in Appendix).

One thing to find out is why did the Muslims in your area settle in Britain? Some came to Britain because since colonial times Britain had been described as the 'mother country'; others came because they were actively recruited. Cotton and wool mill owners in Lancashire and Yorkshire went to Asian villages to recruit workers after the war. The industrialists regarded them as cheap labour for the unpopular night shifts, but they didn't do much thinking about the sociological affect on Muslim families and their settlement in Britain. What was it like for the workers when they arrived? Many men lived together in crowded conditions, with little sympathy from neighbours and inadequate help with cultural adjustments from the authorities or employers. Many suffered alienation, stress and a feeling of not being welcome.[4] Then later on many workers were laid off and had little opportunity to learn new skills.

These women recount their arrival in Britain:

* * * * *

'I came to England in 1984 when I was sixteen. When I arrived I was very sad. Everything was different—the language, the houses and many other things. I love my own country. But now I am all right and like this place better. My marriage was held in Bradford, and now I am living with my in-laws. I am now OK.'

* * * * *

* * * * *

'I got married when I was sixteen; I didn't want to come to England. I had a very hard time, and I missed my home and friends and brothers. My mother wanted me to be with my husband—he is my cousin. When I came to England I wasn't happy at all, I was alone all day. At first I didn't go anywhere, but after a while I went out and met some people here. I like people here now and have made friends with them. But I still miss my country and my home and my mother very much.'

* * * * *

Across Britain, each Muslim community is unique. Bradford, with over 50,000 Pakistanis, is very different from, say, Cambridge, with an estimated total Asian community of 2,000. Bradford is very different again from some inner London boroughs, which have a variety of well-developed minority communities, rather than one which predominates. Scotland, Wales and Northern Ireland have much smaller communities, mainly in Glasgow, Cardiff and Belfast. Smaller communities are generally less well-organized than larger ones, with less representation on local committees and councils. They may feel more isolated, and suffer more racism than larger communities which have built up support networks, and whose young people are now forming groups to defend themselves.

Within each community, there are huge differences. The main distinction is probably between Arab, North African and Asian; then within the Asian community between Pakistanis, Bangladeshis and Gujerati Indian Muslims; within the Pakistani community between Punjabis, Pathans and Kashmiris and in all communities between those from villages and those from sophisticated city backgrounds. There are many religious differences too within Islam. Another major factor is that there may be Asian Christian communities from Muslim countries now living in Britain. Did you know that there are Asian Christian Fellowships up and down the country and Asian Christian organizations (see Appendix)?

In the following pages we explore what it is to make friends and how, in the process, we start to understand more about our friends' culture and faith. At the same time we may find we learn more about ourselves.

Notes

1. Bill Musk, *Touching the Soul of Islam: Sharing the Gospel in Muslim Cultures*, p. 18.
2. 1 John 4:18.
3. See Paul's argument develop in Romans 2, 3 and 4; 7:14–13 and 14. Compare too with 1 Corinthians 8 and 9.
4. There is a vivid personal account by a Pakistani worker in Alison Shaw's *A Pakistani Community in Britain*, p. 35, which recounts how prejudice and misinformation about the newcomers was widespread; an article in *The Daily Telegraph* in 1963 ran the headline: 'Pakistanis eat cats'. Alison Shaw's book is a fascinating study by a sociologist who got to know members of the Pakistani community in East Oxford.

[2]

Making Friends

'Why do you want to be friends with me?' asked Shabana, eyes wide with astonishment. 'You're English, I'm Pakistani, don't you mind?' It is sadly the case that many first-generation Muslim women in this country have had little or no contact with other communities. Many have suffered so much rejection or cold-shouldering by neighbours or officials that they cannot conceive why anyone who is not from their community could want to make friends with them. It is also true that many live in close-knit communities where contact outside the *biraderi* (clan) is not expected. For many inner-city Muslims, close contact with the majority community is made more unlikely since the 'white flight'. White Christians are among those who have long since moved out of the inner city. Yet some Muslim women are longing for a special friend, with whom they can share their hopes, fears, joys and sorrows.

Most Christians who have been reaching out to Muslim women in Britain for years and years say that the key is true friendship and genuine love. This will involve actually crossing the threshold and visiting people in their homes. Jackie Pullinger reminded a congress in Germany in April 1995 that God commands us to 'Go'. It may be China, it may be Hong Kong, it may be South America . . . or it may be across the road. And sometimes the shortest step is the hardest.

Hard or easy? I was walking down the road one day and I noticed a Pakistani woman on the other side of the road. I didn't know her at all. I smiled at her and she beamed back at me. Before I knew what had happened she had crossed the road and was standing beside me with her arm round me. 'Come to my house' she said. Within minutes I was sitting sipping hot sweet tea and being introduced to members of her family. Her daughter came into the room and I vaguely recognized her. She said: 'I know you. You played your guitar and talked about Jesus to a group from our school last year.' It's amazing how far a smile across a road reaches.

In most English suburban neighbourhoods it is considered to be a virtue that the occupants of the houses maintain their privacy. 'We're friendly round here, but we don't neighbour, you know.' So said my neighbour when I moved into a middle-class suburban area of Britain. Decades ago it was different, and in some areas it still is the case that everyone knows everyone else; people pop in to each other's houses, look after each other's children, do each other's shopping in times of illness, draw each other's curtains when they're away. It's what sociologists call 'community'.

Have you heard people say: 'Asians keep themselves to themselves'? What they mean is that they cannot recognize anything familiar in the lifestyle of Asian communities who seem willingly divorced and separated out from the majority community. The reality is that Asian families are much more open to outsiders than most English families. On high days and holidays, such as *Eid* (festival at the end of Ramadan), even non-Muslims are invited in to share in the celebrations. Compare that with western Christmas Day with our invisible 'Do Not Disturb' signs. Asian families are ready to share food, hospitality, gifts, and often open themselves up in deep friendship with those who genuinely want to build bridges.

For anyone who wants to build friendships with Asian families this whole issue of visiting, receiving visits and hospitality is a fundamental one. I have been humbled by the level of openness and welcome I have found among Asian families when I have visited, but I have also been saddened to hear accounts or see for myself efforts at friendliness from them towards English neighbours being rebuffed. Of course it sometimes happens the other way round too. But when a member of a minority group is rebuffed, there is more than personal rejection; there is humiliation suffered on behalf of the minority community too.

One lady I visited was very shy with me. Only after much gentle chatter did she open up and answer my offer to help teach her English. She shrugged her shoulders and said: 'What's the point? I tried once to speak at the Post Office but they laughed at me.' These rejections, coupled with experiences of outright racism (see Ch. 6) help to explain why Asian communities often find it necessary to stick together in a hostile or bewildering environment.

How vital, then, it is for Christians of whatever background, to throw caution to the winds, let down the drawbridge and cross the threshold into our Asian neighbour's home.

Discuss

- *Is your neighbourhood 'friendly'?*
- *Do you find it easy to 'cross the threshold'? - Do you think you need to be an outgoing person to do so?*
- *Have you ever visited a Muslim home? - If so, what were the unexpected joys and what were the unexpected difficulties?*
- *Have you ever felt vulnerable and like a fish out of water?*
- *Have you experienced being a stranger in a new place or situation? - If so, how have these experiences helped in your friendships with Muslim women living in but not born in this country?*

Be humble, respect, receive

A note for those of us who are white, British-born Christians: vulnerability can actually be a key to unlocking hearts. When we go onto someone else's home ground we become learners. This can be enormously helpful when we are reaching out to those who are in the minority in this country, and who are usually in the vulnerable position. When those in the strong position willingly become listeners, learners and receivers, they grow in knowledge and understanding. This helps to foster a right relationship based on mutual trust and respect.

Westerners can be greatly enriched by their friendships with Muslim women. At festivals, such as *Eid*, special foods are cooked and large numbers of visitors are welcomed. Could this be an opportunity to learn from our Muslim friends how to cook *halva* (carrot dessert) or sweet rice? It's fun doing things with other women and western independent women sometimes miss out on such community activities. We can also be humbled by the help our Muslim women friends offer us when we are in need. Many Christian women have testified that it was their Muslim friends who were most ready to offer comfort and sympathy in a bereavement, coming round, cooking for them, crying with them.

Sometimes it is more blessed to receive than to give. It means giving over the pleasure of giving, to the one who gives to you! See how Jesus approached the Samaritan woman in John 4. He humbled himself to ask her for a glass of water. He allowed her to give to him, before giving her the water of life.

Discuss

- *Can you think of a time when established roles have been reversed in a friendship?*
- *Have you ever been surprised by help or comfort from unexpected quarters?*

No strings attached

Friendship is deeply valued in Muslim culture; a female friend can be closer than a husband. Muslim women prefer personal friendships to one-off encounters and are very open to genuine offers of friendship. Our motive must be love, with no strings attached. If the only motivation is to win the person for Christ, this implies that if they do not convert the friendship is in vain. We will find that in making a genuine two-way friendship, we can share our faith naturally. But first we need to earn the right to speak of our faith. This may mean sitting in our friend's home for many hours, weeks, months and years, accepting the hospitality offered and entering into a real friendship on eastern terms, not our goal-oriented western terms which demand results.

When we enter friendship it is therefore good to envisage a long-term commitment. This is not easy in our fast-moving, dislocated society, where job changes mean people move from one part of the country to another and it is often almost impossible to keep up all the friendships we would wish to. Yet once you make friends with a Muslim woman and her family, you become almost a part of the *biraderi*, the clan. This brings with it privileges and also responsibilities, in a way westerners may find surprising. See the section on *lena-dena* in Ch. 4.

Discuss

- *How much time are you willing to sacrifice in making friends with Muslim women?*
- *What do you think you can give in your friendships?*
- *What do you think you may receive from your Muslim friends?*
- *How can we be sure our motives are pure? How might our national history and social background affect our friendships?*

Why won't you be my friend?

Traditionally, friends are part of the extended family and it is not usual to invite friends home from work or school. When outside friends are made, it is traditional for them to be from the same stratum of society in terms of status and wealth, and also of the same sex and similar age. If you find your overtures are rejected, it may be that they feel it is inappropriate for any of those reasons. Another point which needs to be borne in mind is that in traditional families, the husband needs to be consulted before a woman can feel free to make friends with whom she chooses.

'Without meeting there is no mission!'
(Canon Dr Philip Lewis, Bradford)

We cannot witness to those we do not love, neither can we witness to those we do not meet! Only one white churchgoer in a thousand lives in the inner city. Eighty per cent of British Christians live in suburbia. Yet the vast majority of Muslim women live in the inner cities of Britain. Is there a case for us Christians reversing the upward mobility trend of the 1980s and the white flight from the inner cities by choosing to move into inner-city areas to live in the heart of the community we wish to serve?

How shall we meet?

Jesus met the Samaritan woman at a well—a natural place to meet, though across a huge cultural and racial divide.

Wherever you live, what are your natural meeting points? Buses, school gates, shops, doctors' waiting rooms, the post office, down the road and over the garden wall. Community classes and teaching English at home are excellent meeting points. We can teach English, and also maybe learn Urdu or Punjabi! It really helps to know some basic Asian language, even if not at an advanced level. This section explores these natural meeting points and Ch. 3 explores contacts in work situations.

Visiting neighbours

Many Muslim women will really appreciate a friendly neighbour's visit, especially if they are at home with young children. It's a good idea to check when the best time to visit is, and that the husband is happy for you to go. If your friend's husband is in on his own, it is not the done thing to sit and wait with him for his wife's return. This may be misinterpreted! See the section 'His and hers' in Ch. 4.

As well as at times of celebration (the birth of a child, visitors from abroad, festivals), it's also good to visit in illness or bereavement. Westerners are used to respecting personal privacy in these situations, but it's the opposite in Muslim culture. When visiting a bereaved family it is usual to sit with the family for a couple of hours, showing respect for the deceased and support for the bereaved. It's much more acceptable than just sending a card.[1] Similarly, when someone is ill they usually appreciate people round them. If you know your friend well enough, you can make the tea for her, and maybe do her ironing. Muslim hospitality being what it is, however, she may insist on getting up to serve you. When you know someone well enough you are regarded as a 'sister' so she'll let you serve her.

Language

Have you ever wished you had paid more attention during French lessons at school? Asking the way in Calais when you're late for the Channel crossing soon sharpens up the old brain cells.

Trying to speak a foreign language to those for whom it is their mother-tongue makes you realize how stupid you feel when you can't communicate. Despite a common European heritage between the French and the English, history shows there is still plenty of room for misunderstandings. Just imagine, then, the situation for older Asian women living, though not born in this country, trying to learn and speak English. The linguistic gulf between Urdu or Punjabi and English is huge, as is the gulf in culture, food, dress and understanding. On top of language difficulties, there is the added issue of expressing oneself in public; some Muslim women have little experience of this.

It must of course be stressed that many Muslim women are very competent both in their mother tongue and in English; one cannot assume that anyone who was not born and brought up in Britain has difficulties with the language. Many women who came from East Africa or from cities in the subcontinent or the Middle East are highly educated and fluent in English and are prime movers in their communities. Their world is very different from that of women who came to British cities from villages in Pakistan and Bangladesh and who may not have had much formal education.

Many women from the Mirpur area of Pakistan are semi-literate or illiterate, which of course does not mean they are unintelligent. They have much wisdom in bringing up children and traditional ways handed down over generations. Often women's memories are very sharp and they can hold a lot of information at once; mental arithmetic skills are also often highly developed. Information is passed on by word of mouth. Such women may also not be able to speak Urdu, though they will understand it.

Marion Molteno's book *A Language in Common* (See Bibliography), describes how she taught community English classes to women in the London area from many different language groups. She shows how it is possible to build up warm relationships not on the basis of linguistic fluency, but on a common humanity. She has found that when words failed, human personality and ingenuity stepped in. Many with Muslim friends find this to be true.

Teaching English to speakers of other languages (or Teaching English as a Second Language as it is sometimes known) can be extremely rewarding. Facilities vary across the country: in some inner-city areas there are language schemes which have been operating for many years, whereby unqualified volunteers, having attended a short course, can teach English informally on a one-to-one basis in student's homes, or as assistants in community classes. Some areas require volunteers to gain a basic qualification, such as the City and Guilds Initial Certificate in Teaching Basic Skills (E.S.O.L.). If you are ambitious, you can gain higher qualifications which may lead to job opportunities; further details are available from the organization NATE-CLA (see Appendix).

Learning another language

It is a very worthwhile experience for those of us who want to reach out in friendship to Muslim women in this country to try learning some Urdu, Punjabi, Gujerati or Bengali and see how it feels in reverse. There are local authority classes in the major cities. You can learn for fun or if you are more ambitious you can study for a GCSE. There are various methods; joining a class is a good way; having an Urdu speaker as your own personal tutor is another excellent way. The LAMP (Language Acquisition Made Practical) method is highly recommended (see Appendix).

As one British Asian person said: 'If you lose your language, you lose your identity.' Language is one of the ways into a culture and a people. It is very hard to begin to understand another culture without getting into the language. Translation is all right as far as it goes, but it only provides a pale shadow, a sort of 'second-hand' understanding. Some concepts in one language cannot be translated into another language because in that culture the concept does not exist. Similarly, the same word can have different meanings according to culture; for instance, the word 'democratic' can be translated into German, but in former East Germany (the German Democratic Republic) its meaning was poles apart from the western equivalent. The Arabic word *insha'Allah* can be translated as 'God willing' or 'DV', but is the Muslim understanding of the will of God the same as the Christian one?

It is interesting to note that there are certain words which keep cropping up when we speak with Muslims. One such phrase is *salam'alekum* (peace be with you) as a greeting. The reply is *wa'alekum a'salam* (and also with you). Any Anglicans recognize this? Similarly, the Urdu phrase for 'goodbye' (*Khuda hafez*) literally means 'God be with you'. Did you know the word 'goodbye' is a contraction of the original English blessing 'God be with ye' in the English language too? It is worthwhile learning these words of greeting as they establish a positive start and finish to any encounter with Muslim friends. Another commonly-used phrase is *ma sha'a 'llah*, meaning 'what God has made'. This is important to use when praising or congratulating someone, so that the glory goes to God, rather than to the person.

Lorna Hayward has written a practical guide to the variety of Asian languages spoken in Britain (see Appendix for details). There is also a section on language in 'Honour, shame, saving face and the community' in Ch. 4.

Muslim international students' wives

Throughout Britain, there are Muslims from almost every country in the world who have come to do a course at a British university or to study English at a language school and there are many opportunities to befriend them. Some are here for only a few months, others for a year or several years. Some are single, others are married but have left their family back home, and others again are wives accompanying their student husbands. Since they are only temporarily resident in Britain, they don't expect to join a community of compatriots nor do British issues such as political representation or Muslim schools affect them. Their home country is still their main concern. Some will return to be the future 'movers and shakers' in their country, forming foreign policies, granting or withholding missionary visas, or giving permission for a church to be built.

Modern well-educated, articulate Muslim women may shatter the image we have had of Muslim women, or Muslim society and its rules. While they are in Britain they are eager to encounter many aspects of British life and culture and to meet local people.

International Student Christian Services (ISCS) is an organization which encourages Christians to reach out in friendship to international students and their families. One of their workers gives an account of her own experiences in forming positive two-way friendships with Muslim women students and student wives:

* * * * *

'I met Fatima[2] at a social group for the wives of international students. She was a fully qualified doctor in her own country, but she had come to Britain to accompany her husband who was doing a PhD at the university. We quickly got past the surface to deeper matters, enjoying the opportunity to find out about each other's cultures. "What do English people think when they see a woman with her head covered?" she asked me. That gave me good openings to explore how she perceived British culture. Her impression was that most British were living godless, immoral lives. She saw I was different and I explained how my Christian faith had affected my moral code, my attitude to family life and so on.

'Being a doctor and a little older than most of the other women from her country gave Fatima quite a high standing amongst her compatriots. When there were tricky situations with some of the other wives, she was able to mediate. As trust developed, she and her husband spoke freely to us about the problems in their country, giving us a new perspective on a country much maligned by the western media.

'Our friendship gave us both great satisfaction as we shared many aspects of our lives as wives, mothers of teenagers and educated modern women who saw faith in God as central to life. The nitty-gritty of life (food, family illness, stressed husbands) also formed part of our conversations and laughter was never far away. Never before had I shared myself so fully with a Muslim friend; we were soul mates and I shall always treasure this friendship and pray for the day when the basis of our sharing will be a mutual love for Jesus.

'As other friendships have developed, I have invited the whole family to our home and that is always a very happy occasion. I soon realized that if I took up all the invitations to visit, I would not be able to visit anyone more than once or twice a year—hardly the way to build up a close relationship. So I encouraged other young British mums from local churches to befriend one international student wife. I gave them a few cultural tips to start with and several good friendships have developed. I have found that if I make the introduction personally, student wives are happy to meet someone who is a friend of mine, and I can let it go on from there. One young mum committed herself to visiting an Iranian wife every week. Their mutual affection was evident: "I love her to bits", said my British friend.

'In several university towns there are Wives Groups, some run by the university itself, others by a group of Christian women or a particular church. They provide activities such as crafts, cooking and seasonal events. Christmas and Easter can be opportunities for low-key Christian events. Far from being offended by the religious message, most women are delighted to discover there are actually people of faith in secularized Britain and that festivals like Christmas do have a religious meaning beyond Santa Claus. Wives Social Groups provide a neutral meeting point, from which invitations come to visit students' homes. In the absence of the wider family, these wives feel very alone. Many are lonely and frustrated since they may have had to abandon their career back home and courses are difficult to attend due to inadequate childminding facilities. The opportunity to have an intelligent conversation with someone in their home is greatly valued.

'Many Muslim women feel a spiritual and cultural dislocation when they arrive in Britain and become more devout than they had ever been in their home country. I'm often asked whether the students' wives know that I'm a Christian. I find that quite amusing because religion, God, faith, prayer are so much part of the lives of Muslim women that not to speak of these things would be unnatural. They know very early on I am a Christian and I hope it's clear to them that I respect anyone who is serious about God. One Muslim student asked to be placed with an English Muslim family. The university drew a blank but passed her name on to us! We wrote, explaining that though we were not Muslims, we were people of faith and also understood her dietary restrictions. She responded very warmly and so began a good friendship. I and my Muslim friends have many things in common, but when it comes to religious zeal, they outshine me every time. There are many who really want to worship and serve God. They are not fanatical, or politically active, just devout.'

* * * * *

If you live in a university town or city it's certain that there will be Muslim students or students' wives who are looking out for friends. You may like to contact ISCS (see Appendix) for ideas. Meanwhile:

Discuss

- *Can you find out what groups already exist at the university and whether you can support them? If not, can you help to set one up?*
- *If you are already involved and find you cannot visit everyone you've met, can you introduce other Christian women to some of your friends?*
- *Do overseas Christian students attend your church? Can you offer them hospitality and together pray for their Muslim fellow students?*

Difficulties, misunderstandings and *faux pas*!

Early on, it may seem strange entering someone else's world and one is bound to make faux pas, or be taken aback by different customs. The following examples are of situations which you may have faced (or may yet face) when visiting a traditional Muslim family in their home. Try to imagine each situation and your reaction to it, then try to imagine the cultural or religious reasons behind each situation. Ch. 4 may give you some clues. Frances Iliff's excellent practical booklet Salam Alekum! may provide you with many of the answers too! (See Appendix for details).

- *The man of the house disappears out of the back of the house when you arrive.*

- *You are left alone for half an hour while a meal is prepared.*

- *Your friend Gulshan invites you to come round, saying she wants to tell you something in confidence, but when you arrive you find her sister-in-law and neighbour are there too. Gulshan does not appear at all anxious that they are in no hurry to leave. You are thinking of your dinner in the oven.*

- *You and your husband visit but get separated on arrival.*

- *You and your husband visit but your friend's husband is not in, so you are not invited in.*

- *This is your first visit. You are ushered in and offered fruit and tea, then asked 'How many children do you have?' - You are not married; you say so and following a shocked silence you are asked 'When are you getting married?' - A few minutes later your friend asks you 'How much do you earn?'*

> • *You have never visited this family before, but you have met the woman at an English community class. She asks you to visit her at home. You knock at the door and one of the children comes to the door. He goes back to tell his mother you are there and comes back saying he is sorry you cannot visit.*

Wise counsel?

What happens if you find your friend opens herself up to you and shares deep anxieties, worries, frustrations and doubts? Do you detect she wants you to provide answers to her problems, that you can 'save' or 'deliver' her? What is your reaction as a Christian? What do you say or feel if she indicates she is frustrated with her lot, and is thinking of abandoning her faith and/or culture? Is this a God-given opportunity to share your faith with her? Can you provide answers to her problems? Are you the most appropriate person to do this? Do you really understand her situation? Are you forming a healthy two-way relationship or are you encouraging dependency?

Notes

1. See the section 'Sitting and Being' in Ch. 4.
2. Not her real name.

[3]

Professional Points of Contact

'Oh no, it's that Indian family again. I can never understand what the woman says.' This doctor's receptionist may not be alone in her lack of understanding of Asian people. There is still a long way to go in training professionals and their staff in this area. Health care professionals, teachers, solicitors, social workers and many other professions now deal with clients from many different communities. You may be a Christian woman in a profession which brings you into contact with Muslim women. What are your experiences?

Being a professional usually means you cannot form a relationship of friendship. Has this frustrated you? Or have you been able to come alongside a Muslim client and offer support and comfort, even offered to pray? Have you been frustrated by missed appointments[1] or by an apparent distrust of authority? Have you been challenged or impressed by family and ethical values?

The following sections touch on just four secular professional areas: education, health, social services and community work. This is a huge area, and one cannot hope to do justice to it in a book of this kind, but it is important to raise the issues. Please fill in the gaps according to your own experiences. You may also like to discuss the issues with fellow professionals. Why not get together to pray for Muslim clients and their families?

Education

Some Muslim parents find it difficult to relate to schools. Bilingual liaison teachers may help to explain the system, providing dual text booklets and visiting parents at home, but many are still worried about their children's education. Many fear that their girls will be corrupted at mixed schools after puberty, so they favour single-sex Muslim schools. One argument for Muslim schools is that they provide education for girls from very strict families who might otherwise be debarred from attending school at all after the onset of puberty. Single-sex Roman Catholic schools are highly respected; although they do not teach Islam, they teach respect, modesty and faith in God and standards are usually high. It is secularism, rather than Christianity, which Muslims fear most.

Some of the issues which cause difficulties for the parents of some Muslim girls in mixed schools are swimming, clothes worn for sports, whether to veil, friendships with boys, school trips and personal development classes, where the facts of life, 'safe sex' and abortion are discussed in mixed groups. Other worries include racist bullying and religious education. Of course, some of these issues may also concern Christian parents. It is not only Muslims who prefer single-sex education. Ch. 9 tells the story of an Iranian family who fled persecution and settled in Britain. They became Christians, but that didn't mean they became English; they too were very dismayed not to be able to send their daughter to a single-sex school.

However, some girls do not want to go to Muslim schools as they fear this will cut them off from the wider world. Some parents also want their children to mix with the majority community.

Religious education, school assemblies and festivals in a multifaith context are much-debated and thorny issues. Suffice it to say that there is a whole spectrum of thought among Christians, Muslims, members of other faiths and those of none. Some Muslim parents and some Christian parents want separate assemblies and/or separate R.E. classes for each faith. Other Christian parents do not want any other faith than Christianity to be part of the syllabus. Yet other parents regard school as providing information which will prepare their children for the world outside; they believe that nurturing their children in their own particular faith is the responsibility of parents and church/mosque/synagogue/temple. Most young Muslim children are raised in the faith through parents' teaching at home and Qur'anic instruction after school. Teaching methods are very different at mosque school; the children are taught to memorize the Qur'an, strict discipline is maintained and the teacher respected (or even feared).

I always remember an Indian Christian friend (brought up in a Hindu family) telling me that it was through the multifaith R.E. syllabus that she became a Christian. She was given information about the major world religions and she had the freedom to make an informed choice. It became clear to her through her inward searching and prayer that Christianity and the person of Christ stood alone and was the truth. The Evangelical Alliance pamphlet *A Celebration of Faith* quotes a Christian head in a multicultural school as saying: 'Christianity will stand up against other religions in honest debate. And children do not necessarily choose to follow Christianity if it is the only faith they are taught about.'[2]

A Christian R.E. teacher in a multicultural school was challenged by her Muslim pupils' enthusiasm for the subject: 'My Muslim pupils actually want to learn about religion and take the G.C.S.E. exam. I find it hard when they answer questions and I think "this is so similar to what I believe". Our shared heritage of the Old Testament prophets and the Law means that when I'm teaching about Islam I have to keep telling them: "Remember this is Islam, not Christianity!" They are devout, keeping the fast during Ramadan and very able to express their faith.' Many teachers will concur with this experience of Muslim children's religious awareness, in sharp contrast to that of their nominally 'Christian' peers. One teacher reports that when she was teaching about fasting, she asked 'What is Lent?' and got no answer. She then asked 'What is Ramadan?' and the Muslim pupils' hands shot up. Their detailed explanations jogged the memories of the nominally Christian children who vaguely remembered something about eating pancakes and giving up chocolate.

Two excellent publications for Christians grappling with these issues are the above-mentioned *A Celebration of Faith* by EA/EMA and the Spring 1993 issue of the magazine *Racial Justice* titled 'Education and Racial Justice Now'.[3] The former gives practical guidelines to Christian parents on how to face these issues, when to make a stand and when not to. It helpfully explains that some issues are cultural rather than religious and do not compromise our faith. The latter explores the Education Bill and racial equality. It contains a particularly useful two-page spread of books and resources.

Education and Politics

One sore point for some Muslim (and no doubt some Christian) leaders may be the unrepresentative structure of the SACRE (Standing Advisory Council on Religious Education). This body advises on the implementation of the Agreed Syllabus for R.E. and on assemblies and worship in each education authority's schools. It is made up of four groups: teachers, councillors, the Church of England and 'the rest'. This latter lumps together Roman Catholics and Nonconformist churches along with Muslims, Sikhs and Hindus.

✂ ─── ✂

Discuss

- *If you are a teacher or have children in a multicultural school, how do you handle these issues?*

- *Mr Mukadam, Muslim parent-governor at Birchfield School, Aston, Birmingham said: 'In the primary school, let us teach their own faith first.*

Once they have confidence and a good understanding of that, then they can learn about other religions.'[4] *Do you agree?*

- *What benefits can you see in multifaith and multicultural education for children living in today's society?*

Health

Hospitals

Some Muslim women find hospitals very daunting places to be. Even for someone who is fluent in English and who knows the system, it is often hard to keep up with and understand what doctors, consultants or nurses are saying. It is an alien environment, yet one which most Muslim women are likely to encounter, particularly the maternity wing. Depending on local provision, Muslim women's particular dietary and religious needs may not be well catered for. Another difference not always understood by hospitals is that when a Muslim woman is very ill or in hospital for some time, her culture regards it as normal for her to have frequent visitors. It is anathema to be alone, particularly when you are ill. In the Indian subcontinent, families often camp out in the hospital grounds, bringing food during the day and sitting with their relative until nightfall. Obviously the system is different here and a compromise can often be worked out.

There are certain taboos, such as undressing in doctors' surgeries or hospitals, which can cause acute embarrassment.

In many Muslim cultures women do not undress for medical examination. When it is necessary for a woman to deal with a man in some situations this can make her feel very uncomfortable. Embarrassment is sometimes caused when, in the absence of an appropriate interpreter a woman's son has to interpret for her. One Libyan woman in London needed her eleven-year-old son to interpret for her during the delivery of her baby. Not surprisingly, this was too much for him and he passed out.

Surgeries

Many Muslim women prefer female GPs, gynaecologists and dentists. In many inner cities there are practices where one or two doctors are Asian and therefore understand the culture and speak Asian languages. Other practices have liaison workers who are bilingual. Understanding of the particular issues affecting Muslim women as regards smear tests, breast cancer tests, birth control, pregnancy, ante- and postnatal care and abortion is essential if there is to be a good relationship between patient and clinic. Many women feel under pressure and rushed when they go to the doctor and may be bewildered by the red tape and paperwork often involved.

A white Christian doctor who lived many years in India comments that many of her Muslim patients talk freely to her about their faith and their desire for God to heal and help them. She notes that preventive medicine and a fatalistic belief in the will of Allah are not easy bedfellows, so treatments are not always followed as doctors might like. Muslims know Jesus to be the Healer, and often regard him as a *pir* (holy man). Families quite often approach Christian ministers instead of doctors to ask for prayer in Jesus' name.

Health Visitors

There must be hundreds of Christian women health visitors who in the course of their work visit Asian homes and so meet Muslim women in a professional capacity. Different cultures means different ways of bringing up children. One health visitor commented that the practice of spoon-feeding babies of thirteen or fourteen months was backward; they should be using a knife and fork. Toilet training often comes later in Asian families, which is sometimes not understood at nurseries. Women who have just had babies are particularly sensitive to inappropriate comments, so special care and understanding is necessary when crossing cultures.

If you are a health visitor, you may recognize aspects of the following accounts of two visits by an English health visitor:

★　★　★　★　★

It's a . . . girl [5]

'A young mother gave birth to her eagerly awaited third child. Tears often follow a birth, but her weeping went on and on. Grief mingled with her growing love for this third daughter. Whom could she talk to without causing more tears for others or criticism of herself? I was willing to listen, so she began to express her feelings.

'She had felt so certain it would be a boy; special prayers had been said and a holy man consulted. A celebration had been planned, but now there were to be no guests, no special food, no special clothes. The grandparents obviously favoured the boy cousin born a few weeks before. Now there was just the anticipation of saving money for three dowries, preparing for the heartbreak of giving away her precious daughters to other families and being bereft of the comfort of a son who would stay with her in her old age. She feared that a fourth child might only add to the distress by being another girl. I could only listen and be the friend she needed, and pray that there would be a time to tell her about my own faith, and the love and comfort that it offered.'

Who is there to love me?

'Any young mother kept awake all night by an asthmatic baby feels tired and in need of tender loving care herself. One particular young mother told me: "Well, it's not just the baby, it's so many things. I'm so unhappy. I long to see my own mother but everyone says that my mother-in-law is now my mother. She is the one who should tell me what to do. She blames me for my baby being ill and won't help me look after him. She won't let me go out anywhere except to the doctor's or the hospital. She swears at me in front of other people. My husband says he loves me but he tells me I should respect her and do as she says. We have started to have arguments and he has been hitting me. How can I think of her as my mother when my mother loves me and she seems to hate me? She never even hugged me when I had the baby; she doesn't comfort me when I'm sad. My husband takes her side. Who is there to love me and give me a hug?"'

* * * * *

Discuss

- *If you are a health visitor or district nurse how far do these stories concur with your own experiences?*
- *Have you felt perplexed or even angry at times when faced with quite different customs in bringing up children? - How do you handle these feelings?*
- *Have you ever come away from a household and thought: 'Well, I wouldn't have done it that way, but it seems to work!'?*
- *Do you see ways in which you can share the knowledge you have learned (or may learn) from other cultures with your professional body?*

Special needs

Having a child with, say, cerebral palsy, is a challenge for any family, of whatever culture or religion. As in some western families, there may be an element of shame or guilt felt by a Muslim family. For some Muslim families, this is felt particularly acutely by the mother, who may be blamed for bearing a child with impairments. Many families show great love and care towards such a child.

A young English woman working as a physiotherapist in a multicultural inner-city school for children with special needs, acknowledges the great value of Asian outreach teachers who serve as go-betweens and translators for Muslim families. She recognizes that it is sometimes not appropriate or acceptable for Muslim parents (especially mothers) to come to the school and meet the teachers or health workers on unfamiliar ground. It is especially important that the parents feel comfortable and can have their child's treatment and education explained in their own language, if they are not fluent in English, and through a mediator if they feel nervous at approaching the professionals. A mediator is particularly helpful since in traditional Asian culture a conflict situation is most often approached through a mediator, rather than head on, as in the West.

Discuss

- *If you are a health worker or teacher with children with special needs from Muslim homes, what are the major factors you feel can influence the child's progress at school, physically, mentally and emotionally?*
- *What is your experience of the children's families? What are the ways you have found to put the children's care in the context of their home background?*

Mental health and Muslim women

According to research by Dr Veena Soni Raleigh of Surrey University, the suicide rate for Asian women between 1988 and 1992 was twice the national average. Research also shows that in the same period the suicide rate for sixteen-year old Asian girls was four times the national average.[6] Ratios were lower for Pakistani and Bangladeshi women over 24 than for Indian women of the same age, but not at 15–24 years of age. What are the causes of this despair?

The Commission for Racial Equality funded a research study of sixteen Asian women in Bristol who had suffered from depression[7], which revealed the extent to which their depression was intensified by their difficulties as ethnic minorities. During interviews these women explained how unremitting racial aggression made them prisoners in their own homes, yet their complaints to the council about this and intolerable housing conditions often fell on deaf ears. They felt lonely and isolated, with extended family members too far away to offer support, and they felt unable to express their needs to English-speaking professionals. Some women could not cope with the pain of separation due to immigration difficulties (see Ch. 6), and others became depressed when they first arrived: 'When I came here, that first day, everything seemed very strange to me. Where we live in Pakistan there's a lot of coming and going. You see everybody. Here, once you're inside these four walls it's like you're in prison, you don't see anyone or speak to anyone . . . I guess my illness began when I came here.' Another woman's depression started when her husband was killed in an accident. While still in a state of shock and grief and least able to cope, a deputation of neighbours came round and told her to 'go back from where she came from'. Social obligations and pressures from within the community, looking after children and problems with in-laws were also contributing factors.

The Inner City Mental Health Project where Asian link workers liaised between the women and their GP practices and ante-natal clinics was a great help. Several women also stressed the positive effect of their faith. One woman explained: 'I try to pray five times a day because that gives me more support than all these tablets I take.'

Many Muslim women believe their depression and fears are caused by *jinn* (spirits). Ch. 7's section on the evil eye and the world of folk Islam explores this spirit world further. Muslims believe there are friendly *jinn* and evil *jinn*. An evil *jinn* can cause mental illness or other misfortunes; if friends or family members have a row each side fears that 'magic' powers will be used as revenge. Dr John Bavington, former transcultural psychiatrist at Lynfield Mount Psychiatric Hospital, Bradford, West Yorkshire comments that many patients who believe *jinn* to be the cause of their distress can most often be clinically diagnosed as suffering from schizophrenia, delusional beliefs and ideas, dissociative state (hysteria) or epilepsy. Those suffering from severe epilepsy are sometimes taken to Muslim 'holy men' who beat them to exorcise the *jinn*.

Philip Lewis gives the example of a 29-year-old unmarried Muslim in hospital under sedation for depression. 'She had felt herself ugly and fat, which triggered further bouts of frenzied eating thus deepening her self-contempt. Her elderly parents considered she was possessed by an evil spirit, like an aunt, who similarly remained unmarried . . . Her younger sister, Jameela, was able to understand why

Parveen was depressed, rather than possessed, and her help was enlisted to build up Parveen's self-confidence and self-worth. It was felt that to pray for exorcism would simply be to collude with her parents and sister-in-law in an explanation which trapped her into supposing she could not be married.'[8]

Discuss

- *If you are a worker in mental health services, have you come across cases like these? How have you responded?*
- *Did your professional training include transcultural issues?*
- *As a Christian, what do you think is the link between mind, matter and spirit in mental health?*
- *How do you relate the stories of Jesus casting out spirits to the cases you meet every day?*

Social Services

Two comments from professional social workers can guide our approach here.

One young Pakistani Christian woman, who has worked in a women's refuge, stresses the need to provide a listening ear and maintain a non-directive approach: 'It is important to listen out for the issues and not to make up women's minds for them. Don't patronise. If they think it's right, for example, to go home to a violent husband, it is their decision, their life, their choice. Another point is that prayer is so important. One can do acts of kindness, but they may be totally inappropriate due to a lack of understanding of the culture.'

Similarly, Bassi Mirzania, with a wealth of social work experience behind her[9] has this to say: 'Attitude plays a big part, how we look at people, what tone of voice we use with them, what sort of courtesy we are prepared to give to some and not to others, whether we respect them or not. We should not underestimate such a woman just because she cannot speak English; she may be very intelligent. The job of the genuine social worker is to empower the recipient. If an effort is not made to understand the person before a judgement is made, it may bypass their real needs. All social workers should keep in mind that their job is dependent upon the recipient's needs, not the other way round!'

Let's imagine a fairly typical case. Parveen[10], a 34-year-old Pakistani Muslim woman, is referred to social services. She has left her husband after years of dissatisfaction; he is fifty years old with a morose personality; she is very young at heart and full of life. He has sometimes been physically abusive and kept his wife strictly in *purdah*[11]. He has made all the major decisions and she has never developed to her full potential, either in her emotional or social life. Finally, having been accused of flirting with men, she is physically attacked by male relatives (to preserve the family honour). After years of acceptance, she suddenly 'snaps' and leaves home. In leaving home, she also leaves four children whom she dearly loves. Her overriding desire is for freedom. But what kind, and how will she find it?

Social services pick up the case and she is referred to a women's refuge. She is fortunate enough to be in an area where there is an Asian women's refuge, run by and for Asian women. However, the next dilemma is that the women running it are young, westernized, fully conversant with western culture and some are radical feminists. She is attracted by their free thinking, but slightly uneasy too. What about her family? What about her children? How will she cope on her own, as these women seem to do?

Having spent the past eighteen years as a married woman in *purdah*, only going out to shop and visit relatives, she is woefully ill-equipped for a life without a male to protect and provide. The council house which is made available to her is like a prison. She feels that she has exchanged one form of imprisonment for another. Before, the 'four walls' of *purdah* had at least been familiar and comfortable and, above all, she had never been left alone. From the day of her birth to now she had never been faced with bearing the responsibility for her own life. The solitude and isolation of being separated from her family now is worse than any anguish she had experienced in her unhappy marriage.

How can she be empowered to make an appropriate decision as to how to live? What has the state to offer? What can social services offer? Are there other options? What is the future for someone like Parveen?

Community work

Youth and community work, community relations work, community projects in inner cities are often set up with funding from local and central government and secular agencies, regeneration funds or European Community money. Council community centres, drop-in centres, women's centres, parent-and-toddlers groups and many other projects are often major points of focus and empowerment for those living in our fragmented inner cities. Christians working in such projects may at times feel frustrated by the lack of freedom to witness to their faith, especially when the needs presented are so obviously spiritual ones. Yet those who persevere can play a vital role in bringing Christianity into the secular arena. We may work alongside Muslims (and Hindus, Sikhs, Jews and, of course, atheists!), with the opportunity to put forward the Christian view on ethical and other issues. In social and community work, religious faith is almost a taboo; in community relations, faith is integral to ethnic identity so the 'English' community is Christian, the Pakistani community is Muslim. In working with the community we have an opportunity to represent Christianity as it really is, in trying to live out in practical ways Christ-like lives. Clients of other faiths may be surprised that some of the service providers have high moral standards and integrity which they do not find often in secular society. They may also find that these practising Christians have a love and a compassion which is hard to explain, but which comes from the very nature of Christ.

'Then the King will say to those on his right, "Come, you who are blessed by my Father; take your inheritance, the kingdom prepared for you since the creation of the world. For I was hungry and you gave me something to eat, I was thirsty and you gave me something to drink, I was a stranger and you invited me in, I needed clothes and you clothed me, I was sick and you looked after me, I was in prison and you came to visit me . . . I tell you the truth, whatever you did for one of the least of these brothers of mine, you did for me"' (Matthew 25:34–36,40). This passage has a vitally important message for us as we seek to serve our fellow human beings: it is Christ himself whom we are meeting when we reach out to others; God incarnate is the one whose feet we wash. This is a revolutionary (even seemingly blasphemous) concept for Muslims, yet it is at the heart of the gospel. Let's pray that whatever occupation we have, whether secular, Christian or home-based, our love for Christ will be what motivates our service of our Muslim clients, friends or neighbours. If we do, the difference will be evident.

You may like to refer to the section on Christian community projects in Ch. 8.

Discuss

- *How do you express your Christian faith in your work with the community?*
- *What are the specific issues when working with Muslim women in the community?*
- *What is the difference, in practical terms, between tolerance, acceptance and promotion of a group's religious beliefs?*

Notes

1. See Ch. 4: 'The guest is king!'
2   Quoted from *A Celebration of Faith*, see below.
3. The pamphlet *A Celebration of Faith* is available from the Evangelical Alliance. Tel. 0171-582-0228. The Spring 1993, issue No. 19 of *Racial Justice* 'Education and Racial Justice Now' is available from ECRJ (see Appendix for details.)
4. Quoted in *The Independent*, 15 February 1996.
5. Ch. 5 explains the preference for girls in more detail.
6. The Radio 4 *PM* Programme on 31 October 1996 quoted research by Dr Veena Soni Raleigh: Institute of Public Health, Surrey University, Guildford, April 1996.
7. *The Sorrow in my Heart: Sixteen Asian Women Speak about Depression.* Commission for Racial Equality: London, 1993.
8. From an unpublished paper by Philip Lewis: 'Cross-cultural counselling: how far should you enter the world of assumptions of those for whom demon possession *(jinn/bhut)* is still part of the explanatory system?'
9. Her professional career is outlined at the end of the Foreword.
10. Not her real name.
11. See Ch. 4 for an explanation of *purdah*.

Part II

Islamic Ways of Life

Part II

[4]

Crossing Cultures

'However well intended, the judging of one culture by the tenets of another has historically led to much ill-will between people and nations.'[1]

Three notes about culture: Firstly, many of the aspects of Muslim culture explored below are not specific to Muslims only; they may be shared by Sikhs, Hindus and Asian Christians, as well as South American and African cultures. Secondly, it is all too easy to generalize; Asians are always 'late' or westerners are always time-conscious. Often it is personality or temperament rather than culture which determines behaviour. Thirdly, no culture is static; all cultures are to some extent fluid and subject to changes from inside and outside. What is British culture? Is it beef eaters and Morris dancers? Is it Welsh male voice choirs or Scottish ballads? Pop stars and rave parties? Church fetes and amateur dramatics? Guy Fawkes night? Diwali celebrations and multiracial community events? Or is it a mixture of all these? As a multicultural society, ideas of what makes up British culture are changing, just as Asian cultures are changing too, adopting aspects of western culture. Is change a threat?

Jumping to conclusions

It is easy to take a culture at face value. We may see something which is strange to us and which reinforces a stereotype: 'Those poor women who have to put a *dupatta* (scarf) on when they go out.' Or we may misinterpret a comment because we do not understand what lies behind it, as the following example shows:

A Muslim woman, Parveen, asked her Christian friend, Sarah: 'Do your people clean their babies when they change their nappies?' 'Of course we do!' retorted the young mother, thinking this was an extraordinarily insulting question to ask. A few weeks later, she understood what lay behind Parveen's question. She had visited the toilet at Parveen's house and found there was no toilet paper. All she could see was a jug near the toilet. She asked Parveen what this was for and Parveen explained that Muslims wash after going to the toilet. According to Islamic hygiene rules, water should be poured over the area. The use of toilet paper (particularly in a hot country) is regarded as unhygienic.

Discuss

- *Can you think of an instance when you realized you had jumped to conclusions about someone you didn't know very well? (Or when someone else jumped to the wrong conclusion about you?) How did you (or they) come to realize?*

- *Can you think of an instance when someone from another culture made a comment which, on face value, sounded rude? What lay behind it? Think through attitudes you have been brought up with about other cultures. Which ones do you think are based on prejudice or lack of knowledge?*

- *What aspects of the cultures of your Muslim friends do you find a) positive? b) negative? Why?*

- *If you have contact with Muslim culture, is it causing you to reassess aspects of your own culture? If so, which ones?*

The huge issue of faith and culture, of how Islam and culture are inextricably linked is explored in greater depth in Ch. 7. Chs. 8 and 10 explore cultural issues in the Christian church. Meanwhile, here are some aspects of 'Muslim' culture, expressed in Asia, the Middle East and Europe.

Public and private

One major aspect of Muslim (and Asian) culture is that there are two different arenas: public and private. Often we get a distorted picture of Muslim communities because we usually only see the public side, which may be westernized males. The only way to understand and not jump to the wrong conclusions is to get to know a family in the home. There we see a very close-knit, usually highly moral extended family life, with strong community loyalty (though family breakdown is starting to affect Asian families now too). Ch. 5 explores this in more detail.

'Ye monasib nahi'

This Urdu phrase loosely translates as 'it is not fitting/appropriate'. Muslim culture and religion are so bound up with each other that there are many things which western culture regards as normal, but for Muslims are taboo. The mixing of the sexes is one of the most obvious taboos (see 'His and hers' below). Many Muslims follow the traditions of the Prophet Muhammad, which give precise details of how to carry out the actions of everyday life, unlike Christianity. There are details on how to ceremonially wash and position oneself for prayer, how to dispose of nasal discharge, maintain hygiene and many other prescriptions for daily actions (see also Ch. 7).

Honour, shame, saving face and the community

'If it were not for shame, there would be no honest women.' (Muslim proverb).

Muslim culture is based on community living, where the family's reputation and honour (*izzat*) must be maintained.

Honour is a concept which the modern world and western culture has all but extinguished. Yet it is central to Muslim and two-thirds world cultures. As in other aspects of Islamic culture, one's public 'face' must be maintained for the sake of family and community. (See also Ch. 5 for the implications of *izzat* on family life).

Recognizable piety, hard work, wealth, success and age all bring honour. Being unmarried or divorced, poverty, letting down your family or religion or being raped all bring shame (*sharm*).[2] Note the emphasis is on what is seen externally by society, not on the individual's personal responsibility. Some (not all) Muslims would maintain that if a man sleeps with a prostitute he does not lose his honour, for she is nothing anyway in society's eyes. He has not dishonoured his family. Were he to sleep with his neighbour's wife, that would not only be adulterous, but would bring shame because he has broken a social contract.

Shame is a mantle which is put upon others by society; it is totally different from personal guilt, which originates from within. Western cultures are individualistic and guilt-oriented (apportioning blame: 'It's my/your fault'); two-thirds world cultures are group – and shame-oriented (sharing the burden: 'Shame is upon our house'). In Britain, the lives of many first-generation Muslim women are very much influenced by fear of what the community will think. Women who feel powerless in certain areas of their lives can operate control over each other through gossip. One woman told me when she goes out she wears a *burqa* (all-enveloping long coat, with a gauze concealing the face), otherwise her neighbours from the same village would gossip. Her daughters, however, see things differently and refuse to do things they don't agree with, which they see as hypocrisy.

'To make a mistake and admit it is to make two mistakes.' This Middle Eastern saying sums up the philosophy behind shame. The public admission of wrongdoing is considered more shameful than the act itself. To a westerner this may seem like hypocrisy. Westerners think it is better to be up-front and confess. Westerners confront a wrongdoer; easterners try to save his/her face.

Non-westerners are sometimes accused by westerners of being 'shifty'. Yet usually when non-westerners are indirect or indefinite, they are trying to save face. A neighbour may look rather vague and thank you for your invitation, though they have no intention of coming. However, to refuse an invitation is to bring shame on the host.

Discuss

- *Compare western and eastern concepts of honesty and truth.*
- *Your friend complains about her Muslim neighbour: 'I don't trust her. She doesn't look me in the face. I keep asking her to come round but she won't give me a definite yes or no.' How do you respond?*
- *Your friend finally summons up courage to invite her neighbour to a party but complains: 'She said she would come to the party but she didn't show up. She lied to me. I'm afraid I told her I'd felt let down, I was that upset. Now whenever she sees me in the garden she rushes inside.' What would you say?*

Language

This indirectness is often evident in language. We say 'I can speak a little Urdu'. The emphasis is on the subject 'I' and the verb 'can'. The Urdu translation is *'Mujhe tori Urdu ati hai'*, literally, 'to me a little Urdu comes'. This is the passive voice, and is used more often in Asian languages than in English. It describes things which happen or are done to us. The English phrase 'I'm sorry, I forgot' is in the active voice, implying personal responsibility. The Urdu translation involves no shameful confession: *'Muaf kijie; mujhe bhul gae'*, literally 'Please grant forgiveness, to me remembrance was lost.'

Just to make life more interesting, though, at other times language seems all but indirect. 'Why aren't you married?' 'How much do you earn?' 'Bring me that book.' The first two questions may seem nosy or plain rude to a westerner, whose private life is almost sacrosanct, and who never asks directly about social status. Muslims are not so shy of personal details like these, since an individual's identity is bound up in the wider family and community. The third example is to do with linguistics. Traditional British culture brings up children to 'mind their ps and qs', whereas Asian culture emphasizes the attitudes of respect and gratitude more than the actual words 'please' and 'thank you'. These words exist but are rarely used. Instead the verb itself is modified to indicate respect or familiarity.

His and hers

Particularly in the Muslim community, but in Sikh and
Hindu communities too, males and females have very
different roles. Men have overall responsibility for their
family whom they have a duty to support. They make
all major 'public' decisions. Women have responsibility
for looking after their children, husband and home.
Woe betide the husband who tries to interfere in the
kitchen!

The husband has the ultimate responsibility for any of
his wife's activities which go beyond the domestic realm.
We may not realize that what lies behind our friend's
prevarication when we invite her round is not her un-
willingness to continue the friendship, but the fact that
she needs to consult her husband first. She may feel
embarrassed about this and not tell us for fear that we will
be shocked or even that we may try to persuade her to
'revolt' against the system. A friend of mine told me what
happened when a new Muslim family moved in next
door. The wife asked her to visit early one morning when
her husband was at home. My friend went round to find
the husband still in bed![3] He asked her several questions
and then finally declared: 'All right, you can visit my
wife.'

Physical contact between unrelated males and females
is taboo, so it is best not to sit near someone of the
opposite sex (such as on the same sofa). Women should
refrain from looking men straight in the eye. Similarly,
Christian men should avoid contact with Muslim women

and teenage girls. The usual rule is when we visit in the home, women sit and talk with women and men sit and talk with men (in a different room). Sometimes a family is fairly westernized and will not follow these rules, or they may treat us as an 'honorary male', but we cannot assume this will be the case.

Some Muslim families have become used to the western custom of handshaking, at least in public, but if you are visiting a Muslim in their home, it is better that a man should not shake a woman's hand and *vice versa*. If you offer your hand to a Muslim man who has just performed *wuzu* (ritual cleansing of the body before prayer), you are offering to defile him, so he may well decline! Just to make matters more interesting, there are differences in culture across the Muslim world on this and other issues. The best advice is, don't shake a hand unless it is offered to you!

Many Muslim men living in the West understand that a woman who initiates a conversation with a man is not necessarily implying she's willing for sex! However, amongst traditional, non-urban Muslims in a Muslim country, this is actually the signal one would be giving. Some men living in this country do not understand this, or have not fully internalized it. A young female student turned up at her Muslim friends' house one day to find everyone out except an uncle. He invited her in. He was awkward and rather agitated, obviously unsure how to behave. When he started telling her that he enjoyed watching the students playing tennis because they wore short skirts, she decided it was time to leave! He was polite and showed her out, and no harm was done.

Perhaps it was the first time in his life he had been alone in his house with a young western woman and this had awakened fantasies in his mind. A Muslim woman looking on would no doubt have accused the student of 'tempting' him by going in when no other females were at home.

A Christian woman living in a Muslim country once opened the door to find a Muslim man whose family she and her husband knew and trusted, on the doorstep. He asked to speak to her husband. 'My husband is out', she replied, 'but do come in and have a cup of tea'. The man hesitated and looked confused. She took this to be shyness and encouraged him into the house, putting her hand on his arm in a kindly manner. Imagine her horror when after another minute's confusion he suddenly lost control and tried to kiss her. How would you have reacted?

Reflect

- *Bearing in mind the man had genuinely come to see her husband, that he would have left immediately (as propriety demanded) had she not urged him several times to stay, and that he was an upright Muslim with no intention of acting with impropriety, why do you think he made a pass at her?[4]*

- *How do you feel about the treatment your Muslim women friends may receive, as women, from their men folk? How are you treated when you visit? Does the husband talk with you, treating you as an 'honorary male'? Or does he ignore you? How do you feel about this?*

Purdah

'A woman is only ever well inside her house or inside her grave.' (Muslim proverb)

The word *purdah* literally means 'curtain'. It describes the veiling and/or seclusion of women's bodily features from the gaze of unrelated males, and the separating off of the world of women from the world of men. There is a wide spectrum of interpretations of this concept among Muslims, both in Muslim countries and in Britain. *Purdah* actually predates Islam (as distinct from *hijaab*, see below) and according to some Muslims there is no justification for it in the Qur'an or *Sunnah* (customs of Muhammad). Yet the practice continues to be widespread.

For some women, it means staying at home, within the confines of the 'four walls', only going out to visit relatives. In a village in the Indian subcontinent this is not as secluded as it sounds, since the four walls are the walls of the compound; life is mostly lived out of doors in the courtyard, with constant female company. In Britain, however, this translates into staying indoors in a small terraced house, with little female company. First generation migrants to Britain may not realize that in the thirty years since they left their home country, things have changed there too, for no culture is static.

In most Muslim families living in Britain, however, *purdah* is interpreted much more broadly. Social mixing with non-related males is discouraged and the wearing of *hijaab* encouraged, but life generally has much broader parameters than the walls of the house. Girls go to school, some women go to work and there is an ongoing debate among young Muslim women about what *purdah* actually means in a modern British context.

An intriguing insight into the concept of *purdah* was given on 15 October 1996 on a Radio 4 (*PM*) report on Afghanistan. A member of the *Taleban* (extreme Islamic group) which had captured Kabul and ruled that no woman should be seen on the street explained that this was in order to preserve decency and morality. He pointed out the moral decay in Britain by citing the divorce of the Prince and Princess of Wales: 'Both had admitted to having had relations with another; this is a result of your freedom', he told the reporter. Muslims look hard at public morals and don't like what they see in the West. Neither do Christians. Yet the *Taleban*'s extreme approach does not accord with most Muslims' interpretation of the Qur'an, and it is interesting that Iran and other Muslim countries criticized the *Taleban* for bringing Islam into disrepute with its draconian and 'unislamic' measures.

Hijaab

'A woman without a veil is like food without salt.' (Afghani proverb)

Islamic teaching requires women to dress so that only their face, hands and feet can be seen; they should disguise their curves and draw a covering over their bosoms and hair. This is called wearing *hijaab*. In fact, the traditional dress of most Muslim communities has more to do with culture than with Islam. The traditional Punjabi *shalwar kameez* (baggy trousers and tunic, worn by Muslims, Hindus and Sikhs alike) contrasts with the *sari* of Bangladesh, (also worn by Indian Hindu Bengalis) or the up-to-date fashions of Cairo.

Adherence to the Islamic dress code means that Muslims in Britain are more likely than members of other religions to wear traditional forms of clothing, and, if they do wear western fashions, to be more careful about which styles they choose. Young British Muslim girls are developing their own dress codes to reflect their understanding of modern British Islamic culture. They may show their adherence to Islam by wearing large scarves, carefully folded to conceal their hair, and long coats, while their mothers and aunts may still wear the all-enveloping black *burqa* or *chaador* (shawl the size of a sheet).

Confident professional Muslim women who go out to work do not need to throw off the veil to prove their freedom. *Purdah*, as our Muslim friends will remind us, is a heart attitude more than a rule. Colleagues objecting to their wearing the veil do not understand that they have already made a great step in agreeing to work in a mixed environment; the veil is a symbol of a personal modesty on which they cannot compromise. The same applies to teenage girls from strict Muslim families; their wearing of the veil at school is a symbol of their Islamic purity and modesty in the face of western immorality.

Our clothing

Christian women are enjoined to dress 'sensibly' and 'modestly', just as our Muslim sisters are, though we do not have an exact rule laid down[5]. Since for Muslims the outward appearance is regarded as an expression of an inward conviction, it is important for Christian women to demonstrate their understanding of this by wearing clothes which cover arms and legs (loose fitting trousers are fine with a loose shirt). It is rather interesting to note that both Victorian ladies and hippies meet the criteria; the key is: wear it loose and long! It is also important to remember that what would offend a Pakistani Muslim is just as likely to offend a Sikh or a Punjabi Christian. Our great-grandmothers would also no doubt be horrified to see the way we dress today.

If many of our neighbours are Muslims, it is particularly important for us not to jeopardise the witness of our lives by dressing immodestly and thereby confirming our Muslim friends' view that Christians are immoral. When visiting Muslim friends at home, long skirts, loose trousers and long coats, opaque or dark tights and boots are acceptable. (When visiting Arab and most Middle Eastern families, however, it is much better to wear a skirt than trousers). Some nurses or others who wear uniform may find it possible to wear trousers underneath, as their Muslim colleagues do. At Muslim weddings bright clothes are worn. This is an ideal opportunity to wear a *shalwar kameez*, *sari* or *kaftan* given to you by your Muslim friend. If you think that you might be mistaken for a convert to Islam, you could wear a small cross. If you are invited to a mosque, you need to cover your head and wear a long skirt or loose trousers and a long coat.

The following account, by a community worker who lives in a large, multicultural city, illustrates how we don't necessarily have to follow these guidelines too slavishly, nor be too worried about doing the right thing.

★ ★ ★ ★ ★

'I have been visiting Saira and her father Mr Khan for many years on a weekly basis and we have become good friends. When I visit in homes I try to respect people's beliefs so I always dress modestly—no miniskirts, no cleavage! One afternoon Saira called me in great distress and asked me if I could come round immediately. As I was running up the road I passed two young Muslim men whose families I know. They looked me up and down as I passed and I suddenly realized that I was wearing dungaree shorts. They went almost to my knees but they were shorts nevertheless. There was no time to turn back so I carried on my way.

'When I arrived at the house, Mr Khan had popped out to the chemist. I sat in the kitchen with Saira and she teased me about my dress. When I heard Mr Khan returning I leapt behind the breakfast bar in order to conceal my legs. He came into the room and asked me why I was standing where I was. I said I had left the house in a hurry and I didn't want to embarrass him. When I eventually emerged, he roared with laughter. Firstly, he thought my shorts were ridiculous and secondly he didn't know what the fuss was about. 'When you come to visit, I am usually in my *dhoti* (long seamless garment worn by men), and that shows much more leg than you are showing now!'

I learned a lot from that incident. I still believe it is important to dress appropriately and because I live where I work, I have made certain sacrifices in my lifestyle so as not to cause misunderstanding. It is important, too, to be true to yourself and your own background. There comes a point when people know you well enough to accept you for the person you are inside, even though you dress differently or have different customs. You have to work at it, though.'

* * * * *

Discuss

- *How can Christian women demonstrate their personal modesty and moral values? Should we be visibly different from 'the world'?*

- *Is there any difference between i) a Muslim woman who wears the veil outwardly as an expression of her inner morality, ii) a Christian woman who does not wear the veil but has high morals, or iii) a Christian woman who wears a hat to church?*

Food, glorious food!

It never ceases to amaze me that if I drop in unexpectedly at a Muslim friend's house, within half an hour I am usually faced with a wonderful spread of kebabs, samosas and cut fruit, or even a dish of curry and chapatis. The guest must be fed, and the quality of the food reflects the honour of the guest. It's a good idea to arrive on an empty stomach! It doesn't matter if it's three o'clock in the afternoon, a meal will still be offered (though our friends may realize that we have set mealtimes and let us off with a cup of tea, biscuits and a plate of cut up oranges). It is polite to accept food offered, and even if one is not hungry, it is better just to eat a little of it, than refuse it completely and risk offending our hospitable friends. Of course, if there are health reasons why you cannot eat something, that would be understood. Providing food and accepting it is a part and parcel of friendship.

Many Muslims eat curries with their fingers, breaking off one piece of a chapati at a time and using this as an envelope for scooping up the curry. Once you've got the hang of it, you wonder how it is possible to eat curry with a knife and fork! One English woman who had spent years in Muslim countries went to a restaurant in Delhi and asked for her favourite curry. It arrived, complete with chapati, knife and fork. She looked in horror at the waiter and asked: 'I've never eaten curry with a knife and fork before. Can you tell me what to do?' He answered: 'We thought you'd be able to show us!'

As many non-Muslims in Britain know by now, Muslims eat only *halal* (permitted or 'lawful') food, that is, anything except pork and alcohol, and other meat which has not been slaughtered according to Muslim regulations. Everything else, and any food containing non-*halal* animal products, is *haram* (not permitted). Strict observance of these rules means that it is more difficult for Muslims to accept hospitality from non-Muslims than *vice versa*. Even if we tell our friends that we understand their food laws and produce a vegetarian meal, they still may not be able to accept our invitation since we may have used pans which have previously cooked *haram* food. Tea and biscuits containing no animal fat can be offered, as well as fruit cut up on a plate. During Ramadan, no food or drink is consumed between dawn and dusk, so we may be invited to come round very late to share their meal. See also the section on fasting in Ch. 7.

Discuss

- *What comparison can be drawn between the Muslim attitude towards food and friendship and the Christian symbolism of the breaking of bread?*
- *If you visit your Muslim friends during Ramadan, would you accept their offer of food although they are fasting?*

Lena-dena

In Muslim culture, there is a system of give and take (*lena-dena* in Urdu) which operates when an individual or group enters into relationship with another individual or group. When a friendship begins, a gift may be given as a mark of goodwill. On the next possible occasion a gift is given in return. Such occasions include Eid, readings of the Qur'an (*Khatmi-Qur'an*) in a woman's home, the birth of a child, a wedding or a boy's circumcision. At all these times it is customary for friends to be invited and gifts to be given. Each gift should be slightly larger than the one previously received. This puts the recipient in 'debt', thus ensuring the continued giving and receiving of gifts to establish and strengthen the continuation of the friendship. How to respond to the generous gifts showered upon one by one's Muslim friends is a difficult issue. It may be difficult to talk it through with our friends; and certainly to refuse a gift would be quite hurtful. One pointer is that in giving gifts, quantity is often regarded as more important than quality.

The guest is king (or queen!)

'Do not forget to entertain strangers; for by so doing some people have entertained angels without knowing it.'[6] Hospitality is a biblical theme. It is also an essential part of Muslim culture, so much so that Bedouin tribes will take in strangers and feed them for four days without knowing anything about them. As they are their guests, they will defend them to the hilt against enemies who may be pursuing them.

We have already seen how guests are entertained royally with food and drink, even when unexpected and at any time of day. Are we Christians challenged by our Muslim friends' level of hospitality and kindness? Yet Asian hospitality goes beyond the giving of food. I was deeply challenged by the generosity of many Pakistanis I met during my six-week trip to Pakistan in 1989. On one occasion I was waiting for a long-distance coach between Gujranwala and Lahore. A woman came up to me, asked me where I was going, and went away again. After a few minutes she came back, helped me onto the bus and put the ticket in my hand. She would accept no payment for it. She was doing her duty, to show hospitality to the foreigner in her country. I had to compare the treatment I had received as a vulnerable foreigner in Pakistan with the treatment many newly arrived Pakistanis receive here in Britain . . .

One point to note is that our Muslim friends may feel more comfortable as hosts, rather than guests. It is their duty to offer hospitality, and one which they are very happy to fulfil. They are also on their home ground and may feel safer than in a western sitting room in a formal dinner party atmosphere. Are we prepared to receive hospitality and be the guest (traditionally the weaker role)?

The following scenarios concern traditional Muslim families living in inner cities in Britain, rather than well-to-do westernized families living in suburbia, though you may like to discuss in your group how much difference apparent westernization actually makes to customs. Think through and discuss each situation first before turning to the notes at the end of the chapter.

Discuss

Scenario 1:

- *You are planning to go out for the day as a family to visit your friends twenty miles away. Everyone has been looking forward to it and just as you are about to leave there is a knock at the door. It's Fatima, with her sister-in-law and their four children. What would you say/do? What do you think they would do if the positions were reversed?[7]*

Scenario 2:

- *Fatima's mother is returning to Pakistan after a six-month stay. The day before she is due to leave, Fatima rings you and asks you to come to her house the next morning and spend the whole morning and lunch time with the family, before going to Heathrow in a minibus on which they have booked a seat for you. You have already planned a day's shopping and various jobs that need doing, not to mention the family meals and picking the children up from school. What do you do/say? What do you think Fatima would do if the positions were reversed?[8]*

Time, appointments and the filofax

Someone once said that the West has the clock and the East has the time. During my six-week trip to Pakistan I felt myself becoming altogether more relaxed and less time-conscious; I noticed on arrival at Manchester airport that people seemed to be running around anxiously, chasing their tails. Soon, I noticed myself doing the same and within weeks I was leading the same stressful life as before. I felt myself being wound up, like a clock, by the clock! Bill Musk comments on Middle Eastern culture: 'Precision, punctuality and haste are concepts connoting lack of self-esteem. In fact, only minions, slaves and servants are expected to perform tasks at the "time appointed".'[9] Furthermore, there is no concept of 'my time being wasted': 'Interruptions are enjoyed. They are not a "waste" of time, but the treasured highlights which time must serve.'[10]

Reflect

- *Why is it that our lives in the West are dominated by time?*
- *How do you, personally, cope with the 'tyranny of the urgent'?*

In Muslim culture, plans are always seen as subject to God's will. An orthodox Muslim woman would never say, as we might, 'See you the same time next week, then!' without saying '*insha'Allah*' (if God so wills). We in the West know in our heart of hearts that man proposes but God disposes, but don't we still fight it? Our slavery to our diaries or filofaxes may be denying God the opportunity to overrule in our lives. This aspect (and many other aspects) of our Muslim friends' culture is more 'biblical' than our post-Enlightenment western culture.[11]

This attitude to time may also help us to understand why appointments are not always kept. We may regard it as an insult, having fixed a time to meet, if our friend does not turn up. A Muslim, though, would not immediately take offence. She would think, 'Well, Allah has ordained it otherwise.' In practice, an unexpected visitor may have arrived and the first duty is to entertain them, rather than keep an appointment already fixed with someone else.

Sometimes the insult may be felt by our Muslim friend. Appointments are considered to be appropriate only for business, not friendship. Muslim women expect their sisters to visit them any time and do not mind short notice. A Muslim friend whom I invite round for 'a cup of tea, next Thursday at 3.30pm' may feel that she is being magnanimously 'fitted in' to my important schedule, at my convenience. This gives her the impression that my friendship with her is not very important as I can only spare her half an hour or so, before going on to do something else.

This came home to me most vividly when travelling in Pakistan. We arrived one day at a small town. Our host was sitting calmly by the roadside, waiting for our arrival. I asked our guide, 'How did your relative know what time we would arrive?' (We had been travelling for many hours, with several hold-ups and stops to change tyres). He replied, 'Oh, that's no problem. I just told him which day we would arrive. He will have been sitting here all day.' The only thing happening in his life that day was our arrival and he would have scrubbed out all other activities for that day from his diary (if he had had one!)

Here is a true account by a Christian woman in a northern inner city of how much God used her when she least expected it. He arranged her schedule to fit into his:

★ ★ ★ ★ ★

'My husband and son went to a barbecue—some folk from a local church had arranged it especially for foreign students. After a day away in Birmingham I was too tired to go, so I went to bed for a couple of hours. But I was up at 10.00pm when my husband called in with a Middle Eastern family. They sat down in our dining room and soon noticed some small posters on the coffee table. The lady picked one up, and was delighted to see that the central word on one of the posters actually spelt out her own name, in beautiful Arabic lettering. She went on to read all the words of the poster, and was amazed when we told her they were verses from the Bible. They had never realized there were such things as Bibles in Arabic.

'She and her husband wanted to see exactly where the verses came from, so we produced Bibles in Arabic and other languages, which they pored over with great interest for the next half-hour. It was the first time that the lady had realized the Arabic meaning of her name, and she was quite thrilled by this. When they left, they took with them a little New Testament in their own language, tucked into the man's shirt pocket.

'It was a very nice end to the day. If we hadn't been to Birmingham, I wouldn't have been so tired in the evening, and

I would have gone to the barbecue. Then the Muslim family wouldn't have come back to our house to meet me—they wouldn't have seen the posters—and they wouldn't have got a New Testament to read. God is not limited by our plans or by our tiredness—as long as we keep flexible and open to his voice.'

★ ★ ★ ★ ★

Discuss

- *Can you think of times when God has used you unexpectedly, or has changed your plans?*

- *What is your attitude to others if they are late or don't turn up?*

Sitting and being

I've often thought a much better question when we meet someone for the first time would not be 'What do you do?' but 'Who do you be?' Jesus' words to Martha in Luke 10:38–42 come to my mind whenever I feel anxious because of all the things I have to do and so little time to do them in. The washing up's still in the sink, the hall's half vacuumed, I've just remembered the plants need watering, the pan's boiling over, the phone's ringing, and there just isn't time to sit and relax, still less to read my Bible and pray.

Or I go to visit Shaheen, intending only to stay half an hour, since I have a lot of other things to do. I find the room crowded with female relatives, friends and neighbours, sitting in silence. She is crying. Someone explains to me Shaheen's lost a relative in Pakistan. From time to time, someone brings in tea and biscuits; others murmur prayers. Time goes by and before I know it I've been there two hours. Just sitting and being, rather than rushing around and doing is a major feature of Muslim culture. The emphasis is on human relationships, not on activity, on companionship rather than words. Muslim friends are not afraid of silences in conversations, especially at times of mourning, when we all know words are inadequate.

Tell me a story

How many times have you been on your way to do something, or in the middle of a discussion and a thought, quite unrelated, occurs to you, which is from God? Or you go to mend a pair of slippers, which reminds you to go to town to buy some more shoe polish, which reminds you that last time you were in town you met Jane, which reminds you it's her birthday today, so you forget all about the slippers and ring her instead! Call me scatterbrained if you wish, but I think a timely chat with a good friend is worth three hundred pairs of mended slippers!

But what has going round in circles got to do with telling stories? It's to do with thought processes. A circular thought process is indirect. It may have a point, but the point is not aimed at in an obvious way. Muslim thought processes, like those of Jewish and other non-Greek cultures, are usually circular. So were Jesus'. He didn't preach a three-point sermon, but told riddles and parables, raising questions rather than drawing conclusions. A response or judgement is not demanded from the listener; there is no 'position' to defend, no confrontation. A linear thought process, however, involves a logical progression from A to B to C, and disciplines itself to reject extraneous points. It has a goal; it knows where it came from and it knows where it is going. Western, Greek, post-Enlightenment students are taught to stick to the point and not go off at a tangent. We approach a subject directly and try to persuade by logical argument.

Two-thirds world cultures love stories and parables. Yet they are not just entertainment value but a standard means of communication. Muslims follow the stories in the *Sunnah* of how the Prophet lived as a guide for their own lives. Women use stories to teach ideas and values to their children and in sharing and counselling other women.[12] Politicians from these countries often use proverbs to illustrate points (proving that there are other ways to answer an interviewer's direct question than by evasion!) This rubbed off on Hilary Clinton, who came back in 1996 from a developing country to declare: 'It takes a village to raise a child.'

Professor Duane Elmer describes the powerful effect of a story.[13] A member of staff in a hospital in Nigeria is known to be stealing. What to do? Western staff suggest confronting the individual with his misdemeanour. The Nigerian Administrator, however, calmly gathers the workers together and tells them a story about two villages. One of the villagers started stealing from his neighbours and eventually everyone distrusted each other. The next village noticed the decline and saw their opportunity to attack. The village was captured and the people enslaved.

What do you think happened? The stealing stopped! The Administrator knew it was better to approach the problem indirectly through a story; this way the perpetrator would know he had been discovered and yet no one was shamed.

This aspect of Muslim culture is of great relevance when sharing faith. See the section on appropriate communication in 'How not to hide Jesus' (Ch.8).

Discuss

- *Now you've read this chapter, try answering the questions at the end of Ch. 2 (if you haven't already!)*
- *Do any of the cultural points raised in this chapter shed light on any aspects of your Muslim friends' culture which had puzzled you? - Can you talk them through together?*

Resources in cross-culture

If you are interested in delving deeper into this area, you may like to do some further reading on Muslim culture and cross-cultural relationships and/or undertake a cross-cultural study course (see Appendix).

Notes

1. Bill Musk, *Touching the Soul of Islam: Sharing the Gospel in Muslim Cultures*, p. 15.
2. *Ibid.* Ch. 4 'Honour and Shame'.
3. This situation may seem not to fit in with the Muslim concept of modesty between unrelated members of the opposite sex. However, a white woman is sometimes regarded by Muslim men as neuter, rather than female, and treated as an honorary male. Rules of *purdah* therefore do not apply either to her behaviour in his presence or to his behaviour in her presence. In addition, one's bedroom is not such an inner sanctum of privacy in the East as it is in the West. In Pakistan, men and women often sleep in the same room, fully clothed.
4. A similar story to the one above is given in Christine Mallouhi's *Miniskirts, Mothers and Muslims* (see Appendix).
5. 1 Timothy 2:9.
6. Hebrews 13:2.
7. If you (or anyone else for that matter!) turned up at Fatima's house unexpectedly, and friends were expecting her, she would probably ring (or otherwise contact) her friends and say she is unable to come because she has guests. She would not feel bad about cancelling the prior arrangement with her friends; she would expect them to understand (if they are from Asian culture they would understand that if a visitor comes to your house, everything else must stop).
8. If the positions were reversed, Fatima would recognize the importance of the occasion and feel duty-bound to oblige. She would probably arrange with her sisters or sisters-in-law or friends or neighbours to look after her own children after school and overnight if necessary.
9. Musk, *op. cit.*, p. 112.
10. *Ibid.*, p. 113.
11. See James 4:13–16.
12. See three books on storytelling in the Sociological Studies section of the Appendix, by William Bausch, Evelyn Early, and Helen Watson.
13. Duane Elmer, *Cross-Cultural Conflict: Building Relationships for Effective Ministry*, pp. 100ff. I have paraphrased the story.

[5]

Family Life

Phil Parshall comments: 'Having ... been a close observer of Muslim family life for many years, I want to express my opinion that the West has little to say to Muslims on the subject of family life. A so-called Christian nation like the United States with a national divorce rate approaching 40 per cent[1] can only shamefully repent of having strayed so far from biblical norms. The Old Testament has close parallels to Muslim family structures. Arranged marriages, submission of the woman to the husband, the close-knit family, and the extended nature of relationships all bear strong resemblance to conditions in Islamic lands.'[2]

Belonging to family and community

As a Muslim you are not an individual; you are a member of an extended family and a community. As Bill Musk puts it: 'I am' because 'we are'[3].

Traditionally, grandparents, parents and sons, their wives and children live together as one household. When one part of the family encounters bereavement, illness, the birth of a baby or economic hardship, the extended family takes over their responsibilities. Individuals, especially women, are never alone and privacy and independence are neither expected nor prized. The most senior (usually male) member of the family is the head, making decisions and receiving honour and obedience from the other members. Women in particular are brought up to expect that major decisions affecting their lives will be made by others. A Muslim woman's religion is that of her group even if her personal beliefs may differ.

However, there is an increasing number of nuclear family units among the Muslim community. Migration has meant that most families in Britain are separated from grandparents who stayed behind, and many women miss the support of their own parents when faced with difficult decisions and the dilemmas of living as Muslims in Britain. Children of first generation settlers are now beginning to move out and set up their own homes. (This modern trend is also occurring in urban areas of the Muslim world.) Sometimes a married couple is separated for years because of immigration difficulties (see Ch. 6). Traditional fixed family roles are also changing, with more women doing work outside the home.

What are the advantages of the extended family system? Extended families provide an overriding sense of belonging, along with tremendous practical support. Family members are expected to offer and provide financial and all kinds of help and do so without question. Young couples receive guidance and practical help in bringing up children. Women go shopping in groups, children share games, bedrooms and clothes. An uncle will borrow the video, a cousin will borrow the hi-fi, and an older brother will borrow the car. Houses are often jointly owned by members of the family and property is shared among the *biraderi* (clan). Little Iqbal who 'borrows' Jack's bucket on the beach is not stealing someone else's toy; he is used to communal ownership of physical items. Individual possessions are not valued as highly as in western society. This is of course changing as young Muslims grow up in materialistic, self-oriented Britain.

The positive value of support and the sharing of wisdom across the generations is a great force for wholesome living. It compares favourably with the fragmented and broken families of the West. There can be problems, however. The system can provide a potential cover for abuse. The overriding emphasis is on maintaining family loyalty; individuals usually aim to avoid the group's censure. Problems come when an individual makes a bid for 'freedom' or challenges the status quo. Then the offender may be cut off from the clan, which closes ranks. A westerner probably cannot understand the psychological disaster losing one's clan implies. It is to be thrust out into the wide world, become a non-person, lose one's birthrights or marriage prospects (or marriage partner), and sometimes to be cut off from every single relation for ever.

Discuss

- *If you know a Muslim family as friends, how well have you got to know them?*

- *Are they an extended family or a nuclear family? - Do other relatives live nearby?*

- *How does the family function? - Is it obvious who is the 'head'? - What is the wife's role? - Does she work outside the home? - If not, is she happy to fulfil her role as mother and housewife?*

- *In which ways might we misinterpret Muslim families because of our own cultural values?*

- *In which ways might our own family be misinterpreted because of our Muslim friends' cultural values?*

- *Is our friendship with one member of the family or with the whole family? Can we offer family invitations to family events?*

Izzat

As explained in Ch. 4, the concept of *izzat* is central to Muslim culture. It also underpins the whole of Muslim family life. A Pakistani Christian woman comments: 'Muslim women think very highly of their family, where they have come from, their husband, the fact their husband has a good job. The concept of *izzat* means that it doesn't matter if their husband is ill-treating them. It is better to stay at home and die than to leave home and escape.' The burden rests on the woman to maintain the family honour, so that her husband can hold his head high. When things go wrong (such as marriage breakdown) it is the woman who is often blamed. The system of *purdah* (as explained in Ch. 4) is closely linked with the concept of *izzat*; each buttresses the other.

Marriage

The Prophet Muhammad said that Muslims completed half of their faith when they married. All Muslims are expected to marry, unless they are unable to do so for some reason. Islam teaches that when a man and a woman are alone in a room, there also is the devil. The tacit assumption is that sexual sin cannot be resisted in private and that adults need the help of the community in order to remain virtuous. Sexually mature girls are traditionally seen to be dangerously powerful; they can tempt men into sin, or be tempted themselves; therefore they must be married as soon as possible to maintain the family honour. This belief that female sexuality is dangerous results in many safeguards (or restrictions, whichever way you look at it) placed on their movements, from adolescence to middle age.

Usually, Muslims marry according to the system of arranged marriage, whereby the parents choose a partner and offer them to their child. There are many sayings of the Prophet Muhammad regarding marriage; one is that the permission of the woman (and the man) must be given before the marriage takes place. Yet the way consent is 'given' is described in the following tradition of the Prophet (*hadith*): 'The Prophet said: "The widow shall not be married until she is consulted, and the virgin shall not be married until her consent is obtained." They said: "O Messenger of Allah! How shall her consent be obtained?" He said: '(It is sufficient) that she remains silent.'

But what about love, one may ask? 'Love grows, along with respect, as you live together. It is the commitment which makes the marriage work', comments one happily married middle-aged Pakistan-born Muslim woman who met her husband-to-be twice only before they married. They were only left alone for half an hour each time. 'If I had objected, they would not have forced me to marry him. But we got on well and we have made it work. Love has grown.'

In traditional Muslim marriages husband and wife are not expected to develop a high degree of emotional intimacy. Marriage is not expected to be a complete sharing of heart and mind. A woman will usually be much closer to her mother, sisters and female friends than to her husband. Sexual relations in Pakistani villages are not given the priority westerners expect in a marriage. Husband and wife have to find clandestine ways of meeting when they share their bedroom with everyone else! This pattern is of course changing in Britain.

Husband and wife remain closely linked with their parents after marriage. In a dispute the husband will often defend his parents and the wife hers. If the couple live with the husband's parents, the husband may side with his mother in a dispute with his wife. The wife then has to bow to the demands of her mother-in-law. The son may be torn between supporting his wife and remaining loyal to his mother.

Ida Glaser notes that the biblical view of marriage is that of leaving and cleaving. The apostle Paul quotes from Genesis 2:24: 'For this reason a man shall leave his father and mother and be united to his wife, and the two will become one flesh.'[4] This contrasts with the strong mother-son bond which, in the Muslim world, remains after marriage (see also section below on motherhood). If a couple move out and set up their own home, this can bring greater freedom.

Violence within marriage

Domestic violence is sadly a common feature of many societies in the world. It exists in white families as it does in Muslim families in Britain. But are attitudes towards it in both communities the same? When Paul Gascoigne was discovered to have beaten his wife, society's censure bore heavily upon him. In an interview in November 1996, he acknowledged his guilt and declared that he did not blame women's groups for wanting to ban him from the England football team. Yet years ago, in the so-called 'moral golden age' of Victorian England the law would have been on his side. '. . . spousal rape was fully accepted in law as a part of the husband's right. It was legal for a husband to beat his wife as long as it was with a stick no thicker than his thumb.'[5] It seems that 'Christian' Victorian law was not so very different from orthodox interpretations of Islamic law which sanctions corporal punishment of a wife by her husband: 'Allah has said in the Holy Qur'an (Sura 4:34) "that if it appears that your wives do not obey you, first advise them. If they do not listen, give up sleeping and sitting with them. If even now they do not obey or listen, then beat them (lightly). If they begin to obey thereafter then do not try to find excuses to harass them." "[6]

'I was married but it didn't work'

A Pakistani woman who has worked in a women's refuge remarked that 90 per cent of the women she saw said: 'It was an arranged marriage and it didn't work.' Some of these women had only met their husbands for ten minute periods before they were married. 'The next thing they knew, they were the wife of this man, and suddenly they had a mother-in-law who controlled everything. The marriages which do work are those where there is plenty of dialogue and openness. Unfortunately, often in the Muslim community, there tends not to be much dialogue. The men make the decisions, the men do the talking. The women are like pawns on the chessboard; they just move.'

Similarly, a community worker comments:

'We deal regularly with women in distress, usually from unhappy marriages. It is a constant dilemma for us to know how to deal with such situations. As Christians, we believe that marriage is sacred and for life so we always ask the woman what has been done to resolve the situation. By the time she gets to us the situation is often at the irretrievable breakdown stage. At that point I think we have to take the woman's physical safety and mental health into consideration and support her through her decision to leave. Often her feeling of self-worth is minimal and we do all we can to make her feel special.

'The transformation in some women who have decided to leave is quite incredible. They are literally different people. It is like watching a butterfly emerge from its cocoon. It makes me feel very sad that so many marriages end this way. I long for men to change their attitudes towards their women—they too would benefit from this.'

However, another Christian woman who has met many Muslim women in difficult marriages counsels western women to adopt a cautious, culturally-sensitive approach: 'I don't think it would help these women to advocate "women's lib" ideas. They themselves will gradually find the freedom they need. We know that going to the police is the very last thing they would do because of the honour of the family. In one case the community appealed to me to intervene. I hardly felt I had the wisdom to deal with that case.' Family mediation is a very culturally appropriate method of counselling in the Asian community. A mediator can aid communication and help both sides to save face. The Asian Family Counselling Service based in London (see Appendix), offers marriage guidance and support.

Arranged versus 'love' marriages

Arranged marriage is not so much Muslim as cultural. This system regards marriage first and foremost as a contract between two families. It was the norm in Europe until fairly recently and European royal families traditionally had arranged marriages. It is a constant theme of literature through the ages; think of those famous 'star-crossed lovers', Romeo and Juliet, who encapsulate the plight of young people in love but whose families will not allow them to marry. Arranged marriages are the norm in many parts of the world today, including Asia and Africa where people of all religions, including Christians, follow this practice. Anne Cooper points out that the western dating system is a stumbling block, not just for Muslims. What about Muslim converts?: 'Should they stop arranging marriages to cousins and follow the western dating pattern? This form of dating is perceived as highly immoral not only by Muslims but also Arab Christians.'[7]

But what about young British-born Asians who are surrounded by a culture of western sexual promiscuity and independent choice; what do they think of arranged marriage as opposed to dating and love marriages?

Those who accept the arranged marriage system remark that they trust their parents to choose a partner for them, since their parents know what is best for them. And, since it is an arrangement between two families, they do not feel that it is an individual matter; they have fewer expectations with regards to personal fulfilment. Such young people might say: 'If I make my own choice and it goes wrong, I will only have myself to blame. I might regret having rejected my parents' advice'. We may assume parents always advise arranged marriage at an early age, but I have heard of one family where the parents wanted their daughter to continue her education, yet she defied them and went to Pakistan at the age of sixteen to marry her cousin!

Changing trends

Imagine the horror on a devout Muslim parent's face, when they discover their daughter has been secretly dating a boy at school. For some parents, mixed schooling is itself a contradiction of *purdah*, where a girl must not be in the company of unrelated males from puberty onwards. So girls are told to come straight home from school and act modestly.

Some teenage girls lead a double life, managing to hide their clandestine relationships from their parents altogether, meeting their boyfriends at lunch times or after school. This may last a while, but finally the time comes to be married. Some elope or leave home to escape arranged marriage, bringing shame on themselves and their family. They are usually then ostracized from the family, and younger sisters may be treated even more strictly, or married early in their parents' home country, to avoid them following suit. In 1995 there was the well-publicized case of three Glasgow-born sisters who were abducted by armed men on arrival in Pakistan; in 1994 there were 34 cases of actual or attempted abduction to Pakistan.[8]

One young woman who, in accordance with her parents' wishes, agreed to marry her cousin told me of her anguish and tears at her wedding in Pakistan. Eventually she learned to accept him, even love him—'sort of', she added—but she resolved: 'When I have children, no way am I going to force them to marry someone they don't love.' Some boys go ahead with marrying their cousin from Pakistan, but still keep their girlfriends.

Not only do many young British-born girls suffer a generation gap with their parents; they may also suffer a culture clash with their husbands. If their family tradition is to marry cousins[9], they may be sent to a village in Pakistan, sometimes before completing their education in Britain, to marry a boy who has never been to Britain and who has never met an

independent-minded, well-educated young woman. His expectations of a submissive wife who will be happy to give up
education to marry him and have his children may be sadly
dashed. He will arrive in Britain, vulnerable and dependent on
his wife to help him round the system, needing to learn English,
and finding she has a mind of her own. Some men cannot cope
with their own vulnerability in this and abuse their 'headstrong'
young wives, who in turn, find everything about their husbands
abhorrent. Unfortunately, parents do not realize that two cousins who have been brought up in two such different countries
as Pakistan and England, though close relatives by blood, may
be foreign to each other in expectations and outlook. Some girls
live with unhappy marriages, trapped by the knowledge that if
a girl leaves her husband, she may be ostracized by her family
and become totally isolated.

However, many young, thinking Muslims are prepared
neither to acquiesce with their parents' culture, nor with
that of their white peers. They refuse to live a hypocritical
double life, as this young Muslim writer explains:

'It is with great difficulty . . . that I explain to my
long-suffering parent that in 1996, things are slightly
different. We, the Seventies generation . . . are a confused
lot . . . On the one hand, we have absorbed the influences
of our peers, and hope to find that one-in-a-million Right
Person . . . But on the other hand, we live by a religious
code that enjoins celibacy until marriage.'[10]

He notes that since young Muslims have very few role
models, they will have to create them themselves; he suggests
the formation of a Muslim singles group, in the presence of
Muslim married couples, where young people of both sexes

could meet together in a safe environment, in a '*halal*' way. It is extremely interesting to compare this idea with the needs of young Asian Christians to find a suitable partner in a culturally and religiously acceptable manner. Thought is being given by Asian Christians to this issue. Could young Christians of both Asian and non-Asian origin also adopt a similar model? (Here speaks one who was introduced to her spouse through a couple of praying friends. I'm pleased to tell my Asian friends that I had an arranged marriage!)

Some British-born Muslims may be rejecting their parents' cultural values but they are not rejecting Islam. They are not throwing out the religious baby with the cultural bath water. They are maintaining a genuine Islamic identity, whilst rejecting the layers of culture which they believe are no longer appropriate in Britain. As one young woman exclaimed passionately: 'Islam allows the freedom to choose your marriage partner. As long as you are both Muslims it doesn't matter who you are. It's the culture which is wrong, not our religion.'

There have been cases of clandestine marriages, presided over by a Muslim priest, in the presence of loyal witnesses, at secret locations in Britain's inner cities. No members of either family are present, since they have forbidden the match. Often the young couple are both devout Muslims, but their misfortune is to come from different sections of the community. Once they are married, and the parents have come to terms with their anger and disappointment, there is usually the possibility of reconciliation. These conflicts are not necessarily the result of living in a western culture; there are, and always have been such cases in Muslim countries.[11]

In Pakistani and Bangladeshi villages, traditionally a girl is married soon after puberty, and many first-generation women now living in Britain were married according to this custom. Their daughters cannot be married before the age of sixteen in Britain, of course, and the age at which Muslim girls marry is continuing to rise. Research shows that in 1991 almost 30 per cent of 25–29 year old second-generation Bangladeshi women were still single.[12]

Discuss

Try answering the first five questions in the following list from three different points of view: western, traditional/rural Muslim and British-born Muslim.

- *What are the advantages of 'love' marriages? - What are the disadvantages?*

- *What are the advantages of 'arranged' marriages? - What are the disadvantages?*

- *Do you think romantic expectations in western 'love' marriages are too high? - To what can these be attributed?*

- *Do you think romantic expectations in arranged marriages are too low? To what extent do you think marriage is a social/family contract or a bonding between two individuals?*

- *What about Asian Christian young people who, having become Christians, cannot marry the person of their parents' choice?*

- *Why do you think the television programme 'Blind Date' is so popular? Is there a place for Christian dating agencies?*

Singleness

Unless there is a medical reason, singleness is not an option for Muslims, still less living alone. Islam elevates marriage; Christianity promotes marriage, but allows for singleness too. The example of Jesus Christ is followed by many Christians who want to devote themselves to the single life, able to serve the Lord without family commitments. A single Christian woman may represent a threat to some devout Muslim families, who may fear she will influence the females in the family to desire a life beyond marriage. She herself may for the first time become acutely aware of her singleness and feel a pressure to get married.

Some Muslim women are 'single' through circumstance. A teacher in Bradford comments: 'As you move around, getting to know Pakistani Muslims, you become aware of the many women who are alone with children. There was a husband but he is now with another wife or he has an English girlfriend. His wife has not divorced him and is holding on to her status as a married woman by her fingertips. The stigma of not being married is almost unbearable. I know a dear woman who has brought up three children on her own since her husband deserted her twenty-three years ago, but who a few months ago gave in and married a man who needed a wife to get to Britain. She married him "in order to be accepted in the community".'

Discuss

- *'The Prophet Sallam (Muhammad) said that a woman who dies unmarried . . . will get the status of a martyr.*[13] *How do you square this hadith with the social stigma of singleness?*

Divorce

Did you know that divorce in Britain was not even legalized until 1857? Even when it was granted, a divorced woman lost her legal rights and status, and even worse, her children.[14] Wives were regarded as a husband's property, part of his 'goods and chattels'. The seventeenth-century writer Samuel Pyeatt Menefee's description of how women were bought and sold like cattle is graphically described in a disturbing book called *Wives for Sale*.[15] Yet, thankfully, times have changed! In British law, women now have equal rights in marriage, divorce and custody as men.

Though we have the law's protection from discrimination in marriage matters, can the law save us from unhappy marriages? Presently, western-style 'love' marriages are not faring too well statistically. At least one in three in Britain ends in divorce. The divorce figures are much lower for Muslim arranged marriages in the UK, though divorce is on the increase. According to the Office for National Statistics, in 1996 one in ten children in the South Asian community lived in one-parent households.

In Muslim countries which apply the law according to the Qur'an, Muslim family law says that divorce is allowed. The man can give *talaq* (divorce) by saying 'I divorce thee' three times to his wife, over a minimum period of three months. A woman, however, is not permitted to give her husband *talaq*. This means, if it is the woman who wishes to initiate a divorce, she must gain the permission of her husband, who must then divorce her. If he will not do this, she must ask her parents to persuade him to do so. Yet, her parents may decline to do this, wanting to avoid the shame and dishonour their daughter's divorce would bring on them. If it is a cousin marriage, the girl's parents are also under considerable pressure from the boy's parents, who are their close relatives.

Is it easier to divorce in this country than in Muslim countries? Living as a member of a beleaguered minority here in Britain discourages many women from breaking out since their only security is within the community, however cloying that may be. A woman who is divorced by her husband in Pakistan would usually be accepted back into the bosom of her parents' household, despite the disgrace. Here, however, a woman may have nowhere to go. She has to bear the shame on her own shoulders, and rely on the State for support. This support may provide for her financial and housing needs, but not for her emotional needs.

Young women growing up in Britain are conversant with the system, more independent than their mothers and more able to stand up for their rights. Yet are they any better off? There have been many cases over the past decade of young British-born girls divorcing or leaving their husbands, and *vice versa*. But it's not plain sailing. There is of course the civil divorce procedure. This procedure offers equal rights. However, this is almost irrelevant to a Muslim woman who has been married not only civilly, but also, more importantly to her community, in the Muslim way (*nikah*). Among her community, the Muslim marriage and divorce system is regarded as more valid than the British civil system which is only adhered to as a legal formality. So even if she gets a civil divorce, she is still no better off if her husband does not grant her a Muslim divorce. Without being granted *talaq* she would not be able to remarry another Muslim; her only option would be to marry a non-Muslim according to civil law. If her family refuses to support her she may be no better off than older women in Britain whose parents are 'back home'.

Discuss

- *Compare the Muslim and Christian views on divorce. What do you believe, as a Christian, about divorce?*

- *A young Muslim woman comes to you and tells you her husband, whom she was forced to marry against her will, beats her frequently and forces her to have sex. She has lived with this for three years. Her parents want her to stay with her husband (her father's brother's son.) She has nowhere to go, is hiding from her husband and wants a divorce. How do you respond?*

- *A young Muslim woman comes to you and tells you she loves another man and wants you to help her get a divorce from her husband whom she has never loved. How do you respond?*

Polygamy

Polygamy has existed throughout history across many cultures. One of its original purposes was to care for women whose husbands had died (often in war) or where a war had so reduced the male population that there were simply not enough men to go round. The Islamic view of marriage primarily as a social contract between families and a way of providing for the female concurs with the practice of polygamy. The western view of marriage as primarily an exclusive sexual and emotional relationship between one husband and one wife, cannot accept polygamy. Christianity advocates monogamy. Paul urges the churches in the New Testament to ensure that their leaders have only one wife.

How many Muslims actually have more than one wife? The Qur'an allows a Muslim man to have up to four wives, as long as he treats them all equally (see Ch. 7). Since in practice this is almost impossible, it is usually only the very rich who can afford more than one wife. What sometimes happens is that a man may marry a second wife if his first wife bears him no sons, or they cannot get along, or he falls in love with another woman. Sometimes the second wife is much younger, either a divorcee or a virgin. In the West, there are some cases of men taking a second wife. This second 'marriage' is not formalised in the Register Office, so it is not recognized legally, since polygamy is of course against the law in Britain. However, the marriage is regarded as a legitimate Muslim marriage by the Muslim community through the religious ceremony (*nikah*). Adultery is a great sin in Islam so any sexual relations with a woman other than the first wife must be sanctioned in public by the Muslim community through the *nikah*. In many cases, the husband continues to maintain his first wife and children, whilst also providing for his second wife, though the second wife has no legal rights should the 'marriage' dissolve.

Islam permits a man to make a 'temporary marriage' with a second wife. In Muslim countries this is usually in the case of war or for the purpose of going on *Hajj* (pilgrimage to Mecca), though this is obviously open to abuse. Some young men may use this as an excuse for one-night stands, though this is not acceptable in Islam.

Discuss

- *Is monogamy assumed in the New Testament?*
- *What would be the position of an African man's three wives if he became a Christian?*

Issues for teenage girls

Did you know that 60 per cent of all Pakistanis and 65 per cent of Bangladeshis in Britain are aged under 25?[16] This is true on a world scale too. 'The "average" Muslim is now an urban teenager'.[17] Muslim youth culture is a big issue both within the Muslim community and in the country as a whole. Here we touch on some of the issues.

'Why won't you accept me?'

> *'For many young second generation Asians in Britain, the experience of being described as "immigrants" or "new commonwealth citizens" is alienating. How long will we suffer the stigma of being outsiders? I am British, Britain is my home.'*

More profound than any culture clash or generation gap within Asian families is the alienation many young British Asians feel in society as a whole. The heart cry is: if we're born here, why doesn't society accept us as British? The term 'British Asian' encapsulates their identity as British, from an Asian background. These two concepts are not mutually exclusive!

Discuss

- *What goes to make up a person's identity?*
- *What is the difference between belonging to a country and having a cultural background?*
- *What is a multicultural society?*
- *How would you describe yourself?*

'They don't understand!'

Shaheen is sixteen, speaks broad Lancashire, watches *Neighbours* (and Indian romantic films) and is computer-literate. Her mother is thirty-six, speaks Punjabi, watches Indian romantic films (and *Neighbours*, which she turns off if it gets rude) and has never been near a computer. She remembers with fondness her childhood feeding the chickens and drawing water from the well. She can't understand why Shaheen wants to work in a bank.

Growing up in today's secular Britain, Muslim girls are faced with a myriad of dilemmas and opportunities. The generation gap common to all cultures is exacerbated by an additional cultural gap between parents and children. Efforts made by parents to bridge the gap by taking their children to their home country several times during their childhood help to put children in touch with their roots, but do not solve the conundrum, as this teenage girl points out:

* * * * *

'I have been torn between two countries. Pakistan, where people do not accept me because I have been brought up in a different society. England, where I have grown up, where I will always be an outsider, a "black". It is hard being a British Asian, but we have learnt to cope. I wonder about the day when my children ask me where they belong. What shall I say?'

* * * * *

Some parents, feeling alienated from a bewildering, seemingly decadent society, hold on to their memories and traditions as a security for their own future, and as a means of saving their daughters from moral decay. This approach, whilst psychologically and culturally understandable, may create huge resentment in the girls, especially where there is no opportunity for open discussion between family members. This young Asian girl describes her feelings:

* * * * *

'When you're a teenager your parents watch you closely and you have hardly any freedom. You sometimes lie to your friends when they ask you to come out. When they talk about their boyfriends you feel lonely and you want somebody special in your life. You despise your brothers because they have more freedom. You feel like you're a bridge between two countries, two banks which will never meet, two cultures that will never merge. You feel like a bridge and everyone is walking over you.'

* * * * *

Yet is bicultural living necessarily a 'problem'? Muslim children are often quoted as being 'torn between two cultures', but what is less often referred to is the extent of their bilingual and bicultural living skills. Bob Hitching suggests: 'It may well be . . . that children grapple in different languages with different issues. . . . family issues may be dealt with in one language and all issues relating to their public world in another language.'[18] Many young Muslim women are far more mature, well-balanced and self-aware than their white counterparts, precisely because they have had to think through issues of identity at a much more profound level than their peers. They may move through complex stages before they reach harmony: from total rejection of their parents' culture, to total rejection of British culture, through to a critical appreciation of both their parents' and modern British culture. It may also happen in the other direction, and for some, harmony may take a long time to reach. Like culture itself, this process is in constant flux.

Teenagers in a secular world

The process of secularization in the western world has profoundly affected Christianity. But so has it affected Islam. Bob Hitching asserts: 'Islam . . . is secularizing at a high speed. The ultimate destiny of the Muslim world is to be like the Christian world, nominal and secular.'[19] Muslim communities are not immune from issues such as moral relativism, abortion, contraception and 'safe sex' and these are current real-life issues facing Asian girls in Britain today.

Muslim leaders are struggling to reverse the scourge of secularization which has affected Islam in Britain, and many young Muslims are joining this growing trend towards islamisation. In some universities and colleges, members of lively, zealous and missionary-minded youth organizations outnumber those of the Christian Union. Both evangelical Christians and revivalist Muslims are emphasizing the fundamental core of their faith; they want to strip away all historical cultural baggage and resist corruption from contemporary, secular, relativist society. They are thus rejecting culture and espousing 'pure religion'. Is this to be applauded? Is it a threat? Is it a stage in their search for identity? If so, what kind of dialogue can there be between young Christians and Muslims? What would British Asian Christians have to share in this dialogue?

Discuss

- *In what ways has the process of secularization over the past fifty years affected western Christianity?*
- *How has secularization affected girls from Christian families, growing up in British inner cities?*
- *What do you think attracts some young British Asian women to become Christians?*
- *What do you think attracts some young white women (sometimes from Christian homes) to become Muslims?*

Motherhood and children

'A man came to the messenger of Allah and said, "O messenger of Allah! Who has the greatest right that I should keep company with him and be kind to him?" He said, "Your mother." He said, "Who then?" He said, "Your mother." He said, "Who then?" He said, "Your mother." He said, "Who then?" He said, "Your father." ' This well-known *hadith* underlines the great respect in Islam for the role of mother. Another *hadith* quotes the Prophet telling a would-be fighter to stay with his mother 'for Paradise is beneath her feet.'

Motherhood follows marriage as night follows day in Islamic culture. A woman of twenty-five is expected to be married with children by that age. A childless woman is regarded with pity and may be ostracized by the community. Once a woman gives birth to a boy she feels secure, since traditionally the son will provide for his parents in their old age, and also there is no danger that her husband will remarry. Not surprisingly, much female religious expression focuses on sex and fertility (see the section on folk Islam in Ch. 7).

A mother commands respect in the home and exercises authority over domestic details. 'Being a mother means that her responsibility is definitely at home and that's where her respect and honour come from', explains a Pakistani Christian woman who used to teach English to Asian women. 'That was their first responsibility, to be mother and wife, so anything else, such as staying on after the English class I taught had to come second. Some of the women were frightened of their husband; they were being controlled. They see their main role in life as looking after the children and they do a really good job at it.'

Muslim culture, like many two-thirds world cultures, prefers sons. Traditionally, sons stay with (or near) their parents after marriage, and have a duty to provide for them in their old age. Daughters, however, will leave home and become part of another family. They produce a financial burden for parents who follow the dowry system.[20] Sometimes, the pressure to bear a son is so great that women try time after time, only to produce a string of (beautiful) baby girls. Attitudes are changing though, as they have in Britain over the past hundred years.[21] (See also the section on Health in Ch. 3).

The mother-son dependence is both ways: it is often the mother who has the final word regarding her son's selection of partner but a mother depends on her sons to speak on her behalf into the male realms of power. One mother of five who had left her husband and found herself unable to cope on her own, looked to her youngest child, a seventeen-year-old boy, for support.

Mother-in-law jokes seem to be international. Traditionally, a girl goes to live with her husband in his parents' house. If she is the wife of the youngest son, she is in the lowliest position and may be given the least popular tasks. A mother-in-law can wield a considerable amount of power over her daughters-in-law. After a life of being a daughter, young wife and daughter-in-law herself, she can finally exercise influence over others. She may view her daughters-in-law as rivals for her sons' affections. This is the cause of much inter-family feuding. Not all mothers-in-law conform to the stereotype, of course, and more and more young couples are moving out of their parents' households to set up on their own.

There is no such thing as a solitary mother in African or Asian cultures (unless she is a single mother, and cast out from the community). Three Pakistani sisters, married to three brothers all share care of each other's children. If a visitor comes, one cooks, the other looks after the older children, and one breast-feeds her baby. Meanwhile, next door, a young English mother struggles to cook, clean, wash and iron, whilst looking after her three children under six. She's new to the area and her parents are far away. She sometimes feels like tearing her hair out. Next door but one, a young sales executive kisses goodbye to her toddler, leaving her in nanny's expert care.

Motherhood is regarded in Islam as a career in itself. A woman may work if she wants or needs to, but she should always put her family first. On her way home from work, an English Christian woman popped in on her friend, Salma, who greeted her with: '*Aye, aye*', (come on in), come and sit down. Drink this tea. I feel so sorry for you Christian women (she meant English women) who have to go out to work in the day and cook for your families at night. You must get so tired.'

In Muslim communities there is not as strict a social segregation between adult and child as in western society. Women usually bring their children along on visits and in social settings, such as wedding receptions, the children play freely in the gathering. In traditional Muslim culture, children are brought up with few toys; at a very early age they learn their gender-specific domestic tasks: girls learn to cook, look after younger siblings, and clean the house. Little boys are allowed to roam further and are often treated indulgently by their parents. Young children are regarded as innocent and are often not disciplined. However, as children develop, more and more duties (and restrictions) are placed on them, so that by the time they reach adulthood, their life is intrinsically woven into the extended family system. In western culture, the opposite is true; adolescents are given more and more freedom until they gain full adult independence.

Within the family there is a structured hierarchy; older brothers and sisters are role models for younger siblings. In Urdu, an older sister is called *Baji*, the *ji* being a term of respect. Respect for elders is an integral part of Muslim culture. Young people's disrespect for authority, which seems such a part of modern Britain, is viewed with disdain by Muslims (and with dismay by Christians.) A visitor to England was shocked at the behaviour of English children on the street. 'In my country, any adult can discipline any child if they see them doing something wrong; it's not just left up to their parents. Here if you did that, the child would probably swear at you.' Unfortunately, Muslim children growing up are following the same trend as their white peers. This is worrying Muslim elders in Britain. How can they save their youth?

Discuss

- *Compare the status of motherhood in Muslim and western culture.*
- *What would you say to a Christian woman who, when asked what her profession was, apologized: 'Oh, I'm just a housewife and mother.'*
- *What points of contact are there for married Christian and Muslim women with children?*
- *What role does your extended family play in your children's lives?*
- *How do you react when you see a three-year-old Muslim boy defying his mother and getting away with it?*
- *How do you react when you see older children (of any background) being rude to adults? - How far should we control or punish children?*

Care for the Elderly

Asian and African cultures revere the elderly. There is no such phrase in the Urdu language as 'silly old fool' or 'old codger'. The only adjectives which would be used with 'old' or 'elderly' would be 'respected' or 'wise'. In Asian extended families the grandparents play an important role in the bringing-up of children and in giving general advice. Yet, some families in Britain are beginning to follow British patterns.

There are now homes for Asian elderly people. This would be unheard of in traditional Asian society where children expect to look after and provide for their parents in their old age. Disintegration of the family and the welfare system in the West are changing the dynamics.

Imagine you are an elderly English widow living in inner-city Birmingham whose family never visits you. You 'keep yourself to yourself' and regret the days when you could go to the corner shop for tripe. The neighbourhood's been 'taken over by these Indians', and you don't want to mix with them. Your next-door neighbour is a Muslim woman, whose elderly parents live in a village in Pakistan. One day you see her crying as you pass her in the street. Against your better judgement you ask her what's wrong. She hurries inside without a word. Feeling rebuffed, you forget about it, thinking 'she can't speak much English so I won't be able to talk with her anyway.' The next day her husband comes round with a huge dish of curry, saying: 'Thank you very much for being so kind. My mother-in-law is very ill in Pakistan. My wife is very worried. Please come to our house and have some tea.'

Reflect

- *How do you think this relationship might develop?*

- *Do you know of Muslim families, and of elderly widows with complementary needs, like those above? - Can you help to bring them together?*

Women's Work

There is a whole spectrum of attitudes to Muslim women and work, ranging from a very strict interpretation of *purdah*, through to an attitude of encouraging women to pursue a satisfying career and seek promotion. According to statistics, three-quarters of Pakistani and Bangladeshi women of working age in 1995 were neither employed nor looking for work, compared with the national average of a third.[22]

However, many young Muslim women who have grown up in this country have high aspirations. They are doing far better academically than their male peers. In a group of sixteen-year-old Muslim girls, it is quite typical for several to aspire to jobs such as airline pilots, accountants, doctors and other such professions. Often families are supportive of their girls, allowing them the opportunity to train in their chosen profession and start their career, before marriage. A good education can increase the prospects of a good marriage and therefore a husband who will be able to provide for his wife (and family) for the rest of her life. If anything should happen later on, a woman will have her education to fall back on. In some families, though, further education is seen as a hindrance to marriage prospects, as an overqualified wife may scare off potential suitors. Sometimes a woman will train and work for a few months before marrying. Traditionally favoured professions in Pakistan have been teaching and medicine.

A young Pakistani Christian woman comments:

*   *   *   *   *

'At times I have observed that young Muslim women have
wanted to continue in their education and career, but have
not been allowed to. To work and live on your own in a town
is seen as suspicious; nobody can keep an eye on you. The
trust isn't there. A number of my Muslim female peers have
obtained good qualifications and then married straight away,
without being allowed or encouraged to work, thus reducing
their long-term job prospects. On the other hand I have met
women who have continued to work after marriage, though
this is more common among Sikh extended families than
Muslim. In these cases, the daughter-in-law is given all the
support to go out to work to keep the money coming in. This
is not cultural, but a financial necessity, since she may be the
best qualified to work and support the extended family.'

*   *   *   *   *

In Muslim countries too there is a variety of attitudes
towards women and work. There are many female scholars,
professionals and some notable politicians in Muslim countries. As with all other issues surrounding Muslim women
and their lives, it is impossible (and inaccurate) to generalize
about Muslim women and work.

Except in highly industrialized parts of the Muslim world,
relationships and families are still held as priority, especially in
the lives of women. British-born seventeen-year-old Waheeda,
who works in her father's shop says: 'You get peace in Pakistan.
Here everyone is working twenty-four hours a day, it's hard
work. There, people can relax if they have a bit of land and
grow crops.' A young man compares life in Pakistan with the

four years he has spent in Britain: 'Here everyone is motivated by materialism, always working harder to spend money. In Pakistan it hasn't become materialistic yet. Maybe one day it will.'

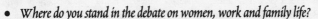

Discuss

- *Where do you stand in the debate on women, work and family life?*

- *Do you agree that 'everyone is motivated by materialism'? - Has materialism hit the church?*

- *Do you have Muslim women colleagues? - How do they juggle home and family?*

- *Now you've read the whole chapter, refer back to Phil Parshall's comment right at the start. To what extent do you agree with him?*

Notes

1. Now, around two out of three American marriages fail. (Source: *Focus on the Family*, United Christian Broadcasters, Stoke-on-Trent, UK., November 1996).
2. Phil Parshall, *New Paths in Muslim Evangelism*, p. 69.
3. Bill Musk, *Touching the Soul of Islam: Sharing the Gospel in Muslim Cultures*, p. 45.
4. Ephesians 5:31. Issues of the status of women and Muslim marriage are explored in Ida Glaser's and Napoleon John's book *Partners or Prisoners?* (see Appendix).
5. Bob Hitching, *McDonalds, Minarets and Modernity*, p. 63.
6. Maulana Ashraf Ali Thanvi, *Bahishti Zewar* (Heavenly Ornaments), p. 474.
7. Anne Cooper, *Ishmael My Brother*, p. 154.
8. According to the charity Reunite.
9. The tradition of cousin marriage guarantees a safe match and keeps wealth within the extended family.

10. From the article 'Angst on the way to the altar' by Amil Khan in *Q-News* (16–22 August 1996).

11. See p. 167 of Alison Shaw's *A Pakistani Community in Britain*.

12. *Social Focus on Ethnic Minorities* (Office for National Statistics, 1996).

13. Thanvi, p. 470.

14. See section *The Basis of Staying Married* in Hitching's *McDonalds, Minarets and Modernity*, p. 63ff.

15. Samuel Pyeatt Menefee, *Wives for Sale: An Ethnographic Study of British Popular Divorce* (Oxford, 1981). The front cover of this book depicts a broadside printed in London c.1832: 'A particular and merry Account of a pretty young WOMAN, who was sold to a gallant young Fellow, for FIFTEEN sovereigns, and a Dozen of Wine, this Morning, Together with the Wedding SONG.'

16. Figures from the 1991 Census.

17. Hitching, p. 18.

18. *Ibid.*, p. 35.

19. *Ibid.*, p. 18.

20. The dowry system is nowadays being challenged by many British Asians who see it as an outmoded custom with no religious basis.

21. See Menefee, The fourth verse of the wedding song (see above) demonstrates the preference for sons in nineteenth century Britain: 'Success to this couple, and to keep up the fun, May the bumpers fly round at the birth of a son.'

22. *Social Focus on Ethnic Minorities* report.

6

National Issues

Social justice

Which camp do you belong to?

- Evangelical Christianity concerned with spiritual salvation?
- Ecumenical Christianity concerned with social action?

Are these mutually exclusive? Indeed, is it possible to have one without the other?

Can Christians and Muslims share common aims and goals in terms of social justice? During the weekend of riots in Bradford in 1995, women of all faiths at Bradford's Millan Centre staged a peace march through the crowd. Are there other social issues, like unemployment or racism or ethical issues such as abortion, sexual morality or euthanasia where Muslims and Christians can join together? Are you aware of the issues which the Muslims in your area face as a daily reality? Do they live in the inner city or have they 'made it' to middle-class suburbia?

Facing the facts

Following the 1991 Census when a question on ethnic origin was included for the first time, the Office for National Statistics compiled a report, confirming that Pakistanis and Bangladeshis living in Britain form a socio-economic underclass suffering a disproportionate level of unemployment, bad housing and poverty.[1] This is not news to anyone who lives in the inner city and knows the conditions many Muslim families suffer. Pakistanis and Bangladeshis have the lowest rates of pay of any similar group. Poverty affects health: Pakistanis and Bangladeshis are the most likely group to have a long-standing illness.

Alienated youth

What does it feel like to be an unemployed Muslim teenager living in inner-city Bradford?

A fairly representative answer would probably come from one of the young Asian men from Manningham, Bradford, who took to the streets one weekend in June 1995, vandalising shops and homes. Why did this happen? At the time the level of unemployment among Asian youths was a depressing 60 per cent, four times that of their white counterparts. Many young Asians reported discrimination: 'If you call the police, and say your name and address, they don't come for ages. You ring some firms and give your name and the job went yesterday . . .' Former Bradford mayor, Councillor Mohammed Ajeeb, pointed out to a meeting of the Race Equality Council in May 1995, that many 30-year-old Pakistanis in Bradford had never actually had a job, and not for want of trying.

There was also a feeling that the majority community was riding roughshod over the sensitivities of the Muslim community. Muslims felt the police had not heeded their campaigns against prostitution in notorious Lumb Lane. Muslim families didn't want to live in this environment, but could not afford to move to 'nicer' areas. Young Asian people interviewed on local television, whilst not condoning the vandalism, understood the feelings of desperation and alienation: 'We want people to listen to us, to what we are saying, what we are feeling. That's all.' This is now beginning to happen. Community leaders, community relations officials and police officers have started to hold meetings where Asian youths (and elders) can have their say. Another sign of hope is that Christians in the area are praying for the peace of the city and its communities.

Discuss

- *What do you think about media coverage of Muslims in this country?*

- *What are your reactions when you hear there has been a disturbance?*

- *How can the cycle of alienation, deprivation and anger be broken?*

- *In what ways can the majority community listen to the Muslim community?*

Racism

'When they throw us out . . .'
'We need to have somewhere else to live in case they throw us out of this country' said a sixty-year-old Pakistani shopkeeper, who has lived in the UK for over twenty-five years. Like many others his age, he is sending money back to his home village to build a house for himself and his family if they need to return. Like many others of his generation, he lives with the fear that 'one day it will all go bad, like in Bosnia. The Christians will fight the Muslims and try to get rid of them from Britain.'

This may seem far-fetched, but a few minutes after visiting his shop I walked past walls daubed with the slogan: 'Blacks Out Now!!'

Facts and Figures

Between April 1995 and March 1996 the police recorded 12,199 racial incidents in England and Wales. This is recognized by the Home Office as an unrealistically low figure, since the majority of incidents are not reported to the police.[2] According to the Home Office, more accurate figures are provided by the British Crime Survey, which estimated that in 1993, though 'only' 9,218 racial incidents were recorded by the police, the actual number of racial incidents against Afro-Caribbeans and Asians (whether reported or not) was 102,000. Of this total, 71,000 incidents were estimated to be against Asians.[3] These figures include all crimes and threats, but do not include 'low-level' harassment such as verbal abuse. *The Observer* published a horrifying catalogue of racial attacks in their 13 September 1992 issue, including numerous murders, stabbings, beatings, arson, repeated harassment and Ku-Klux-Klan activity. One Asian woman was set on fire while waiting for a bus. Mosques and temples are frequent targets, and Asian families in East London regularly get firecrackers through their doors.

A survey in July 1996 by Childline, based on 1600 calls from black[4] children reported that black children suffer street violence and regular verbal abuse throughout their lives. On 26 July 1989, 14-year-old Tahir Akram was brutally murdered by a group of white youths who shot him in the neck from a passing vehicle. The same youths had already shot and injured an African man and another Asian youth, but the police denied racial motivation for the murder. Another Asian youth narrowly escaped death when a car driven by a white man shouting 'black bastard' ran him over. Racism was also denied in the murder of 11-year-old Birmingham-born Tasleem Akhtar in 1989 by a 16-year-old white youth. In 1992 racist playground bullies 'hanged' an Asian youth from a basketball net in Birmingham.[5]

There are, of course, cases of racial abuse in reverse. After years of being on the receiving end of abuse, some young Asian men are forming vigilante groups for self-protection. Sometimes they go beyond self-defence and actively abuse whites. There is also prejudice within and between Asian communities too, so it is not simply a 'white' versus 'black' phenomenon. Many Asians are the first to admit this.

Yet we cannot absolve ourselves from addressing prejudice in our own community just because it exists in others. For racism is more than racial prejudice. Prejudice is a universally common human characteristic. Racism, however, is prejudice plus power. The balance is firmly weighted against minority communities who are often treated as scapegoats for the ills of the country. Institutional racism is buttressed by personal attitudes and conditioning. Whilst racial incidents occur from time to time against whites, they are a fact of life for Asian communities living in Britain. For some people it is an everyday reality. As Jim Wallis of the Sojourners Community says: 'Racism is the ocean we swim in and the air we breathe.'[6]

Racism doesn't hit home until either you have been personally affected, or a friend has, or you have witnessed it happen. A visiting Indian Christian minister and his wife whose door was daubed with racist graffiti, narrowly escaped serious injury when a brick was thrown through the window of their house in inner-city Leeds. The minister's wife had just left the bed where the brick landed.

What about racism against Muslim women? The following event is very vivid in my memory.

No place like home

One day I decided to walk home for a change, to get the feel of the streets I normally drove straight past. I passed the mosque and noticed the door was covered in racist graffiti. I passed rows of terraced houses, some poorly maintained, mostly white families living there. It was what people term 'a rough neighbourhood'. I knew that there were a very few Asian families who also lived in these streets but had never actually seen any Asian people walking around or Asian children playing football.

As I walked, I heard children shouting. I soon came upon a group of about fifteen white children (between ten and fourteen years of age). They were kicking a football up at the top window of the house on the corner of the road and jeering abuse. At first I could not see who they were aiming at; then I saw a woman peeping furtively from behind the curtain of the window. She was Asian. She looked terrified.

I stood, frozen to the spot. Unable to issue an authoritative reprimand, being much too affected to be able to express myself clearly, I stammered out something like 'What do you think you are doing?' Smirking faces, shifting feet. 'We're Paki-bashing, that's what. There's nowt else to do round 'ere. She's only a Paki.'

I was speechless at first. Then I tried to reason with the group, explaining the principles of equality and respect. This did not seem to go down too well and my attempts were rewarded with swearing and abuse. Eventually, the group dispersed and I warned them not to return.

When they had gone, I made my way home, round the corner and down the road. But I could not rest, thinking of that woman behind the curtain. I walked back to her house and knocked on the door. She opened the door, gingerly at first. On recognizing me as the passer-by who had challenged the gang, she burst into tears and ushered me in.

I stayed over an hour. She poured out her story to me. She and her family had lived in that house for two years. Her husband had spent a lot of his savings on an extension to the house, and they had been hoping to stay there for a long time. She told me that they had been victimised by this gang ever since they had moved there. Sometimes it was threats, other times it was damage to property (house and car). They had often kicked a ball up at a window and broken it. The police, when they eventually came, always told the family they would have to bear the costs themselves as criminal damage could not be proven. That was the trouble; nothing could ever be proven. Like the time a firecracker came through the letterbox; and the time the father of one of the boys came round banging on the door and shaking his fist at them, warning that he would kill them if they didn't leave the area. The woman told me they now parked the car three streets away so the neighbours would not know when they were leaving or arriving. The children could not play outdoors any-more as the gang had punched the boy and broken his nose.

This is by no means an isolated incident. A friend of mine and her husband moved away from a white area because a group of children taunted her: 'You can't speak English' whenever she left the house. There are countless other examples of Asian women being targets in their own neighbourhood, many afraid to go out of the home because of racist taunts. Men wearing western clothes may escape such abuse.

Discuss

- *'For evil to triumph, all that is required is that good men do nothing.' Have you ever witnessed a racist incident or heard someone making racist comments? What was your reaction if so? - If you challenged them, how did they take it?*

- *Have you ever caught yourself thinking racist thoughts, or being condescending to a person of another racial background? - How did you feel when you realized? - How did you resolve those feelings?*

- *What would you say to those who say: 'Blacks see racism all over the place; they've just got a chip on their shoulder'?*

- *What would you say to those who say: 'Whites get attacked too, you know. It's usually blacks who commit violent crime?'*

- *How do you think race relations in Britain can be improved? Are you willing to join an anti-racism group? - Is this one area where Muslims and Christians can join hands?*

One day I was visiting Shaheen, when her five-year-old boy came in from the yard, having fallen and gashed open his knee. We took him to hospital and asked the receptionist, 'Which way should Mrs Khan go, please?' A burly man and his friend brushed past us rudely, and one said to the other, 'to the gas chamber, that's where that lot should go'.

I turned and fumed: 'How DARE you say that . . .' at which they were quite surprised. Perhaps they had imagined that they could appeal to me as a member of the 'white club'. I have often noticed that in a mixed group, white people address their racism to other whites, expecting them to laugh or nod knowingly, or verbally agree with the sentiments. Post Office or DSS queues are a good example of this.

Is it possible for 'nice', 'well brought-up' people to be racist? Yes, it is. And it is more difficult to give it the name racism because it is disguised, but racism it nevertheless is. Why do black people find it so difficult to get into golf clubs, cricket clubs, social clubs? Why are they discriminated against in the police service, the prison service and in the legal profession? It is the decision-makers, the managers, the policy-makers in conservative institutions who prefer to keep the status quo.

Some people feel threatened if they themselves are in the minority. Elderly white British people living in inner cities may feel resentful that most of the local shops have been 'taken over' (a loaded term) by Asians. Others bear grudges because of negative experiences. In the middle of a polite, amiable conversation between two English women, one of them suddenly became irate. Her friend had mentioned she was going to visit Pakistan and she retorted: 'Why do you want to go there? We don't want them here!' It transpired she had worked in a shop and found Asian male customers 'so rude'. Her husband could not understand her negativity; the westernized Muslim men he met at the pub (!) and football club were his 'mates'. Negative experiences which are not worked through or counterbalanced produce subconscious prejudice.

But surely it is impossible for Christians to be racially prejudiced? No it isn't. Becoming a Christian does not automatically wipe out years of received ideas and unconscious attitudes. It is particularly difficult to point out racist attitudes to a Christian, who want to believe they are fair-minded, tolerant people. A newly appointed Afro-Caribbean vicar was perplexed as to why the number of people taking communion was lower than in his predecessor's time. Finally, one of his congregation told him that some people could not bring themselves to take communion from black hands. We are probably shocked at this attitude, but is it so very different from never asking Asian members of the congregation to lead prayers or share their testimony ('their accents are rather difficult to understand')?

Discuss

- *Have you ever noticed racism in your own church? - How did you, or will you tackle it?*

- *Has your minister ever preached on the sin of racism, or on racial justice? - Has your church ever studied a series on race issues? - If there are Asian Christian groups in your town, have you ever had a joint meeting? - If not, why not make these suggestions to your minister? -*

- *See the Appendix for racial justice resources and Asian Christian organizations.*

Divided Families

There are countless cases of divided families among the Muslim community in Britain. A major hurdle is the interview process. Both parties to a marriage are interviewed in their respective countries and both have to give the same answers to questions about the relationship between them. Unfortunately, officials often assume that many marriages are 'convenience marriages' entered into only to secure a British passport. Whilst this does sometimes happen (as it does from many other countries in the world, too), it is wrong to equate arranged marriages with convenience marriages. The assumption that genuine marriages are those where a relationship has been built up during courtship invalidates the majority of legitimate, traditional, arranged marriages where modesty demands a lack of intimacy beforehand.

Immigration law demands that a young woman living in Britain, engaged to a Pakistani man living in Pakistan has to have a job, own her own house and have her own bank account before her fiancé is allowed in the country. (This law also applies to a man who marries a girl from abroad.) Often this is difficult as families are not well off and the traditional way is for the young couple (aged, say, sixteen and eighteen) to live with their parents, though this is changing. But they need at least to prove on paper that she owns a house. The extended family may well share houses; an uncle may give his house to his niece so as to comply with the law. British society, not so generous with property beyond the nuclear family, may regard this gesture simply as an underhand way of getting the man into the country, without understanding the far more complex motive of maintaining the centuries-old tradition of 'patrilineal parallel cousin marriage' (to use the anthropological term!) A spouse coming to join his or her partner in Britain is granted an initial twelve-month visa. At the end of this time, the family has to sign a document to say that the marriage is successful. If this document is not signed, the spouse is sent back to his or her country of origin.

One young Asian solicitor who deals with many immigration cases said: 'We sometimes feel helpless. Even when reason and logic show that the applicant is in the right, the Home Office can use its discretionary power to override all the findings. Decisions often appear quite arbitrary.' The following cases are fairly typical. A one-year-old British-born daughter of Pakistani parents went to Pakistan with her mother while her father stayed in Britain working. He visited them from time to time. Eventually she got married there and returned to Britain to settle but her application for a visa for her husband was refused. In the meantime the only job she could find was working in the notorious local onion factory. She visited Pakistan to see her husband on several occasions, and two children were born. After seven years of heartache her husband was finally allowed to join her.

Another woman, born in Britain, went with her parents to Pakistan at the age of fifteen. They settled there and she married, with the intention of returning. When she came home to Britain, her application for a visa for her husband was refused. Officials told her they didn't believe it was a genuine marriage and that she was just trying to bring him into the country. The implication was that she should stay in Pakistan with him. Yet she had been born and bred in Britain, speaking fluent English and she longed to settle down with her husband here. She got a job and a house and following visits to her husband in Pakistan she gave birth to three children. She had to wait eighteen years before her husband was granted a visa.

Another case involved a woman who arrived in Britain to marry her fiancé, but discovered he had an English girlfriend and was not interested in her. She is now happily remarried but still has to face the problem of permanent visa status. Since her visa was dependent on her original marriage, the threat of deportation still hangs over her.

Refugees

Facts and Figures

Britain is one of the most difficult countries to enter the asylum process and achieve refugee status. Out of 43,965 asylum applications in 1995, only 1,295 were accepted by the Home Office. The number of applicants given refugee status between January and October 1996 stood at around 1,100.[7]

Refugees come from all over the world. Today in Britain, there are around 100,000 refugees or asylum seekers. Kurdish refugees number in the 10,000s, and have been quoted as the second largest minority group in Haringey, London. Most have come from villages in Eastern Turkey where everyone knows each other. Being *Alevis* (a sect of Shi-ite Islam), they are rejected by most Turkish Muslims and so are subject to persecution in their own country.

Many applications for refugee status are turned down since it has to be proved that the person is in physical danger if they return to their country. Often the danger is located in one area, or it is the family of the applicant, rather than the government, which poses the greatest threat. Though the danger may not be any less in reality, such cases are regarded as weaker than those which can prove certain persecution on returning to any part of their home country.

Exceptional Leave to Remain ('E.L.R.') is sometimes granted instead of refugee status. This is granted initially for one year, followed by the possibility of extension for a further three years, and a further three years after that.

Benefits such as income support, housing benefit and council tax benefit are granted to anyone who is given either a one-year or four-year leave to remain in Britain. Under the provisions of the Asylum Immigration Act of July 1996, the Government put the responsibility for providing emergency support for asylum seekers on to local authorities, although the guidelines are widely interpreted. Employers are now forbidden by law from employing anyone whose status is uncertain, so many asylum seekers are now literally struggling to survive. At a seminar in December 1996, Christians who had contact with asylum seekers in Britain reported many cases of degrading treatment while in detention. Already traumatized people face the stress of arriving in a foreign culture, being held in detention and carrying the burden of proof; in effect they are guilty until they can prove themselves innocent. Those who have been given departure dates are given plane tickets.

Contact the Refugee Advisers Support Unit at the Refugee Council (see Appendix for address) for further up-to-date information.

There have been a number of centres set up to accommodate the homeless, as with this harsh Bill many are without a means of living. When the Bill was passed, refugee groups estimated that 10,000 people would have no means of paying for housing and food. It is estimated that this number will rise to 40,000 per year in the foreseeable future. A huge burden has now been placed on the voluntary sector.

The Christian response?

This situation provides a real opportunity for Christians to show Christ's love. One refugee family fleeing political persecution in Pakistan noticed that when there was an appeal for clothes by the local Refugee Forum it was the churches who responded. In the summer of 1996 a small group of Christians opened the Care Community Centre at the Bee-hive Centre, Commerce Road, Wood Green, London. It offers refugees help with understanding official documents, benefit and employment advice and translation help for medical problems. For those who are interested, Bible studies are offered, and there is a Sunday afternoon fellowship meeting for worship. There are many other ecumenical Christian groups offering support to asylum seekers. Does your area have such a group? Some churches have a ministry of visiting women in prisons and detention centres.

Building friendships with refugee women is not hard. Loving gestures of any kind, a day out, enjoying meals together and praying with them about long-term health needs are all appreciated as is practical help such as how to use the Underground or understand British bureaucracy. Laughter is cross-cultural and helps relieve stress for those facing an everyday struggle to survive. Language is important too. One Christian woman who understood the Turkish language boarded a bus in London and heard two women speaking in

Turkish. She joined in and the response was overwhelming. The women were overjoyed to be so affirmed. They had lived five years in Britain and had never had the experience of any English face saying 'welcome'.

Bassi Mirzania, writer of the Foreword to this book, arrived in Britain as a refugee. She knows what it feels like: 'They arrive here emotionally and physically exhausted. They will have left behind them their belongings, support structures, identity and status. Arriving here is a cultural shock for them, especially for those women who come from a very sheltered background. Some may give false stories when they arrive here, saying they are single when they have fled oppressive husbands or families, and they may have left children behind. I have been involved in the detention centre at Gatwick where plenty of Muslim families are detained. We need to be sensitive to their dietary, hygiene and clothing needs and preferences and they will appreciate being allowed to conduct their ritual prayers.' Bassi tells the story of Sasha,[8] a refugee from Iran:

★ ★ ★ ★ ★

'A few years ago a young lady came into our church drop-in coffee morning. I realized she was speaking in my own language with her children. I responded to her in that language, but she immediately became very frightened and hurried away. I followed her out, apologized for embarrassing her and gave her my card saying that if ever I could be of help to her, to get in touch.

'Three days later she returned. She told me she and her husband and two children had fled Iran and crossed over into

Turkey where they had spent all their money securing passports to fly on. Back in Iran she had been a teacher, but because of their political views they had been forced to leave Iran.

'At last the way for them to go to Canada seemed to be opened for them, but they were advised not to travel together. So her husband flew first and Sasha and the children flew on another flight later. He made it, but her flight was via Heathrow, where she and the children were caught and detained for travelling on a forged passport. She and her son of two years and daughter of six months were put into a detention centre. With no knowledge of her husband's whereabouts and unable to speak English, she endured extreme emotional trauma. During the several months of detention she was abused, her children developed a skin problem and eventually she was hospitalized. All this time she had been crying for mercy to be allowed to make a phone-call but this was denied her. The housing department finally put her into an inadequate hostel where she shared a room with several other women. There she was robbed and further abused. After three suicide attempts she was given temporary housing and spent her time going round jumble sales to buy bits and pieces for her home. That is when I met her.

'I was very humbled as I listened to her story and we remained in close contact for three-and-a-half years. I put her in touch with a lawyer, and we put the children into a local nursery. As she settled down, everyone came to love her very much. She became one of our most caring volunteers looking after the needs of fellow refugees. One of the local churches accepted her with no strings attached, and gradually they earned the right to share their faith with her.

'Eventually, after many enquiries, we were able to put her in touch with her husband in Canada. Amazingly, he was also getting support from a Christian organization there. It was wonderful to see them share their newly found faith with each other. She eventually became a British citizen and was then able to join her husband in Canada. Before she left, she gathered up all the belongings she didn't want to take with her and gave them all away in the same hall where I had first met her. She left behind her many friends in Britain.'

* * * * *

Here are three more stories from the lives of refugee women:[9]

Parveen's brother became a Christian in Bangladesh. He and his family were threatened by members of the extended family and by the local Muslims who attempted to abduct him. He fled to Britain and was eventually given an indefinite stay visa. Parveen stayed behind in Bangladesh. She had not become a Christian but began to be persecuted because of her brother's conversion. Her in-laws confiscated her pass-port to stop her escaping, but friends got another one for her and helped her onto a plane bound for Heathrow. When she arrived in Britain she applied for refugee status. This was not granted but she was eventually given exceptional leave to remain. She was not allowed to bring her husband over for at least four years, after which time this would only be permitted if she fulfilled the necessary criteria. She managed to get a job and a house and finally, after seven years of separation, he was allowed to join her.

Aisha is the eldest sister of a large family which has migrated to Britain. Her brothers have been persecuted ruthlessly because of their involvement in 'terrorist' activities according to the Turkish police. She has seen so much evil meted out against her family. She tells of her brother being hung with his hands pulled behind his back, because he 'confessed' to being in possession of weapons, though this was not the case. He only 'confessed' to save an older man, a distant relative, from being tortured. However, now Aisha and her family are in Britain they have a new set of problems. Jumping from a world of persecution and deprivation to a world of too much choice and opportunity has been too much for them to cope with. With no minimum wage rule, refugees with little English are unlikely to find any job which pays enough to cover rent and food. One brother has started a business out of his desperation to survive, but some aspects of this are shady. A daughter has run away at the age of sixteen to live with her boyfriend. Another is involved in drugs and Aisha is completely crushed, suffering constant migraines due to the trauma. She has become a Christian and this is now her sole reason to live.

Gyul came to this country looking for opportunities to go to churches. As a little girl she had dreamed that she would some day be in a Christian country. She had seen a vision of Jesus, and was eager to get hold of a New Testament so that she could learn about him.

Many refugees come from countries where the Gospel has been forbidden for centuries. Some have been forced to flee their country because they have converted to Christianity. Others, like Gyul, have a yearning. How many other refugees come to this country with the same yearning?

Discuss

- *As soon as he was born, Jesus became a refugee. How many other biblical examples are there of people fleeing for their lives or suffering injustice? - How would you share the gospel with a Muslim woman refugee?*

- *Among those applying for asylum in Britain are Christians fleeing persecution. How can we respond?*

- *If you live in an area with a large number of refugees, how about visiting the cultural and advice centres[10] and volunteering your services? - Could you visit women in prison or detention centres?*

Notes

1. *Social Focus on Ethnic Minorities* report, 1996.
2. 'Pakistanis are markedly less likely to report threats, even though they suffer a disproportionate number of these. Only 15% of Pakistani victims reported serious threats to the police. Reasons for not reporting to the police vary . . . but negative expectations of the police response seem to figure more prominently for minority victims. . . . Minority victims who report to the police are less likely than whites to be satisfied with the response. For incidents which victims thought to be racially motivated, dissatisfaction was higher still, at 54% for both Indians and Pakistanis.' Home Office Research and Statistics Directorate, 'Research Findings' No 39: *Ethnic Minorities, Victimization and Racial Harassment*, August 1996, p. 3.
3. Figures published in *Taking Steps: Multi-Agency Responses to Racial Attacks and Harassment*: The Third Report of the Inter Departmental Racial Attacks Group, Home Office, 1996, p. 70ff.
4. The term 'black' is used throughout this section in the political sense of members of ethnic minority groups in Britain.

5. *The Observer*, 13 September 1992.
6. Jim Wallis, *The Soul of Politics*, p. 93.
7. Information from the Refugee Council (see Appendix).
8. Names have been changed to protect individuals.
9. Names have been changed to protect individuals.
10. Such as: Kurdish Workers' Association, Green Lanes, Haringey; Turkish Kurdish Centres in Hackney, Haringey, Enfield, Islington and Kingsland Road, Dalston.

Islam

This book does not attempt to give an in-depth theological analysis of the relationship between Islam and Christianity. Other books have done this, notably *Ishmael My Brother* by Anne Cooper (see Bibliography). However, this chapter does cover the basics of orthodox[1] Muslim beliefs and the position of women in Islam.

The Prophet Muhammad

Who was this man? Muslims have a very high view of Muhammad who is held to be *al insan al kamil* (the perfect man). Suzanne Haneef writes: 'He was a devoted husband, father and grandfather, a kind and responsible kinsman, a faithful, affectionate friend, a leader alike in worship and battle, a ruler and statesman par excellence. For the Muslims of his time as well as for the Muslims of today and tomorrow, he was and is and will always be the model: the teacher, the guide, the leader, and above all the conveyor of the Divine guidance, the connecting link with God, and the person whom they love, revere and emulate above all other men.'[2]

Muhammad was born in Mecca in 570 AD. His father Abdullah died before he was born and his mother Amina when he was six years old. Then he lived with his grand-father, the guardian of the *Ka'ba* (the holiest shrine of the Black Stone), who died two years later leaving him in the care of his uncle. As a young man, Muhammad worked for a rich widow, Khadijah, whom he married. Muhammad received his first revelation in a cave in Mount Hira when he was forty. He felt God was calling him to be his Messenger. The central message he believed he should give was the oneness of God; he alone must be worshipped, not idols. Some believed in his prophetic role, but others did not and opposition grew, forcing the prophet and his followers to move in 622 AD to Medina. This year of emigration (*hijra*) became the first year in the Muslim calendar (1 AH) and Medina became the centre of the Muslim community (*ummah*). Later, after a number of battles, the Muslims conquered Mecca and cleansed the Ka'ba of its idols. Muhammad died in 632 AD and is buried in Medina.

Islamic beliefs

- The first duty of a Muslim is to believe and say that God is One: THERE IS NO GOD BUT GOD (*LA ILAH ILLA LLAH*). This is known as *Tawhid*. God is unique, eternal, the creator and sustainer of his creation, controlling the course of this world and our lives. Since God is ONE, anyone who makes someone the associate or partner of God is guilty of the grave sin of *shirk*. Idols and images are strictly forbidden. Pagan believers, idolaters and Christians are guilty of *shirk* in the eyes of Muslims. Sura 5:19 of the Qur'an makes this clear: 'In blasphemy indeed are those that say that God is Christ.' This is also why mosques have no decorations or images.

- The belief in angels as God's messengers, doing his will. There are two recording angels who attend every person, to record their good and bad deeds.
- The belief in God's Books—the *Tawrat* (Torah) given to the prophet Musa (Moses), the *Zabur* (Psalms) given to the prophet Dawud (David), the *Injil* (gospel) given to the prophet Isa (Jesus) and the *Qur'an* revealed to the prophet Muhammad. The Qur'an is the only Scripture accepted as perfectly true; previous books have been corrupted or are not available to us (such as the Scrolls of Abraham).
- The belief in God's Prophets and Messengers. The list of prophets mentioned in the Qur'an includes many of the Old Testament ones (Adam, Noah, Lot, Abraham, Isaac, Ishmael, Jacob, Joseph, Job, Elijah, Elisha, Jonah, Zachariah) as well as Jesus, John the Baptist and Muhammad[3].
- The belief in life after death, resurrection and the day of judgement.

The perfect religion

Muslims believe that Islam is not a religion, it is *the* religion. The Qur'an states: 'The Religion before God is Islam (submission to His Will)' (Sura 3:19). Whilst there are verses which urge tolerance: 'Let there be no compulsion in religion' (Sura 2:256), others suggest forced conversion: 'Fight and slay the pagans wherever ye find them' (Sura 9:4). It is certainly a missionary religion. Furthermore, those born into Islam must remain Muslim; anyone who renounces the faith commits the sin of apostasy. Punishment for this can be imprisonment or even death. Although the Qur'an does not demand the death penalty, there are some *hadiths* (traditions) which seem to advocate it.

Reflect

Think of helpful Bible passages as you pause to reflect on your own faith:

- *Who is God for the Christian?*

- *How do I know him? How would I describe him? Do angels have a role in the Christian faith?*

Some misconceptions Christians have of Islam

Some Christians still think Muslims worship Muhammad. Churches may encourage this thinking. In a young people's service three people were asked to play the parts of a Hindu, a Muslim and a Christian. They were asked the name of the God they worshipped and were told to reply 'Jesus' for the Christian, 'Krishna' for the Hindu and 'Muhammad' for the Muslim. There are no problems with Jesus or Krishna, but for a Muslim to worship any God but Allah is blasphemy and worthy of a death sentence. Muslims believe that Muhammad is the final prophet and messenger of Allah, but they never worship him.

Discuss

- *Can you think of other Christian misconceptions of Islam? How do they come about?*

- *Do you agree with those who say Christians do not need to understand Islam, we only need to understand the gospel of Christ so we can preach it to Muslims?*

- *Did you realize that 'Allah' is the Arabic word for 'God' and that Arab Christians therefore worship 'Allah'? (Though in Malaysia it is banned for the Bible to translate God as 'Allah'.)*

Some misconceptions Muslims have of Christianity

Muslims think that Christians worship three gods: God, Jesus and the Holy Spirit (or even Mary). This is assumed because the Godhead is spoken of as God the Father, God the Son and

God the Holy Spirit. For a Muslim the idea of three separate gods is blasphemous, yet so is it for the Christian. Christians strongly believe that there is but ONE God: 'The Lord our God, the Lord is one . . . (Deuteronomy 6:4). Jesus echoed this more than one thousand years later in Mark 12:28–30. Though the word 'Trinity' does not appear in the Bible, Christians began to use the term to help explain that God is three in one. The New Testament provides some help in understanding the mystery of the triune God.[4]

Jesus features many times in the Qur'an. He is seen as an accepted and honoured prophet and his virgin birth and miracles are recorded. He is even referred to as the Word (*Kalima*), the Messiah (*al Masih*) and the Spirit of God (*ruh'Allah*). It is believed that he ascended and that he will come again, but his crucifixion is strongly denied. The central problem for Muslims is: how could God become a man and how could God die? Almighty God would never allow his prophets to fail, but would rescue them. A more productive discussion with Muslims is not how but why did Christ die?

Sin or shame?

The fundamental difference in belief about sin is summed up as follows: a Christian sins because she is a sinner whereas a Muslim is a sinner because she sins. Original sin is a Christian concept. Sin separates us from God; when we sin, we hurt God and his image in us is marred. Muslims believe when they sin they hurt themselves and incur God's wrath. We saw in Ch. 4 'Honour, shame and the community' how evil and personal morality are external concepts for a Muslim. If a man has not appeared to have committed adultery, he hasn't sinned and there is no need for confession. However, a woman whose hymen has been broken through an accident may be regarded as being guilty of fornication. Islam believes it is the job of the religious system to rule and regulate public behaviour so as to restrict evil (hence the *purdah* system). Christianity teaches that evil originates first in the human heart and that it must be dealt with before it can be effectively controlled in the public domain.

Reflect

- *Look up Hebrews 12:2. The culture of Jesus' time was a shame-based culture. Reflect on the shame he suffered, dying on the cursed tree, outside the city wall. What does this have to say to Muslims?*

- *Can the Muslim concept of shame help to illustrate to our Muslim friends the shame we have brought on God through our sin?*

The Qur'an

In 610 AD in the Cave of Hira, some three miles north of Mecca, Muhammad was spending the night in meditation. There he heard the word '*Iqraa*', which means Read! Proclaim! or Recite! The veil was lifted from the Preserved

Tablet and its contents began to be transferred (in Arabic) to the mind of the Prophet.

Muslims believe that the origin of the Qur'an is divine. The early revelations warn people to turn away from idols to worship Allah, the one God. Other suras (chapters) contain biblical stories and later revelations concern times for prayer, direction of prayer and fasting. Muhammad did not perform many miracles like other prophets, but God gave him the Qur'an, a miracle, since he could not read or write. The Qur'an is not experienced by Muslims primarily as the written word, but as the spoken and heard Word of God in Arabic. It is handled with great respect; never to be placed on the floor and touched only with clean hands. Often it is wrapped or kept on a special stand. Listening and learning to recite the Qur'an from memory is more important than studying and understanding the text. The *hadith* is an oral tradition and encourages Muslims to recite and perform *dikr* (repeatedly remembering and saying the name and words of God out loud).

The Bible and the Qur'an are not comparable. The Qur'an is seen by Muslims as the Word of God, directly descended from heaven, the revelation of God. So we need to compare the Qur'an with Jesus, rather than with the Bible. For Muslims the Word came down and became 'book' but for Christians the Word of God came down and became flesh and dwelt among us (John 1).

Discuss

- *Try to get a copy of the Qur'an. Are there parts of the Qur'an which are true?*
- *How about attending a short Islamics course? (See Appendix)*
- *What do we believe about the revelation or inspiration of the Bible?*
- *How does God reveal himself? Study Hebrews 1:1,2 and 2 Peter 1:20,21.*
- *Where would you start to read the Bible with a Muslim friend? What stories would she know that might be a good place to begin?*

Islamic practices

Islamic practices can be summed up in the five pillars of Islam:

1. To recite the Creed or Witness of the faith (shahada): THERE IS NO GOD BUT GOD AND MUHAM-MAD IS THE APOSTLE/MESSENGER OF GOD. (LA ILAH ILLA LLAH WA MUHAMMAD RASUL U'LLAH). This is spoken into the ear of a baby at birth, and Muslims will continue to recite it in Arabic all their life and especially at the moment of death.

2. To pray five times a day (*salat*). Muslims pray at dawn, just after midday, late afternoon, immediately after sunset and before midnight. In some towns in Britain the mosque calls Muslims to prayer as it does in Muslim countries. On Friday many Muslims go to pray at the mosque. Mosque worship consists of formal prayers and

a sermon by the *imam* (mosque leader). There is no music; the atmosphere is one of utmost reverence and solemnity. The liturgical form of prayer (*namaz*) can be prayed in a congregation or alone; many women perform *namaz* at home. After ritual ablutions (*wuzu*) the prayers proceed with a specific pattern of standing, bowing, kneeling, prostration and sitting. Informal prayers of supplication (*du'a*) can be prayed at the end of these prayers and at any time.

3. To give welfare contributions/alms (*zakat*). Sura 2:177 of the Qur'an says: 'Those who believe, and do deeds of righteousness, and establish regular prayers and regular charity, will have their reward with the Lord.' *Zakat* is a compulsory payment of 2.5 per cent of one's income or savings, cash or gold. It is not a tax as it must be spent on the poor and needy.

4. Fasting (*sawm*). Fasting is obligatory for all Muslims (with certain exceptions, such as the sick, pregnant women and travellers). *Ramzan* (Ramadan) is the annual month of fasting during the ninth month of the Muslim lunar calendar. It is believed that during this time the first part of the Qur'an was given by Allah to the prophet Muhammad. Between sunrise and sunset Muslims should abstain from food and drink (including their own saliva), perfumes, tobacco and conjugal relations. Women who are menstruating are not permitted to fast; they carry over the 'lost' days until after Eid, when they can catch up.

5. Pilgrimage to Mecca (*Hajj*). If possible, every Muslim tries to go to Mecca once in his/her lifetime and

perform the ceremonies required at the *Ka'ba*. Women who go should be accompanied by a male. The *Hajj* is during the first twelve days of the twelfth month of the year. Muslims remember how Muhammad and his followers entered Mecca and destroyed the idols in the *Ka'ba*. The *hadith*[5] say that every step taken in the direction of the *Ka'ba* blots out a sin, and to die there helps to ensure one of heaven.

Discuss

1. *Can you state your belief in one sentence? Is there a biblical verse which can help?*

2. *How do Christians pray? Does it matter when, where or how we pray?*

3. *How could you use the Lord's Prayer to explain Christian prayer?*

4. *What is the Christian teaching on giving? Why, how, when and how much do we give?*

5. *Reflect on the Bible's teaching on fasting. Why do Christians fast? Could Ramadan be an opportunity to discuss the Christian view of fasting with our Muslim friends?* [6]

6. *How might you and your church approach the month of Ramadan?*

7. *Is Lent fasting? Read Isaiah 58.*

8. *How does the Hajj compare with a Christian visit to the Holy Land?*

9. *How important is the Holy Land to our faith? What impact do you think western (especially American) Christian Zionism has on Christian witness to Islam?*

10. *What 'works' can a Christian do to please God?*

Festivals

'*Id il-Fitr* at the end of Ramadan, colloquially known as 'little Eid', is the best known festival in the Muslim calendar, occurring in the ninth month of the year. Hospitality is given, gifts are exchanged, the house is spring-cleaned, everyone has a bath and wears new clothes. A special breakfast is eaten to break the fast and prayers are said at the mosque. Muslims explain it as 'our Christmas' to their non-Muslim friends. 'Big Eid' (*'Id il-Adha*) takes place on the tenth day of the last month and commemorates Abraham's offering of his son Ishmael (rather than Isaac) as a sacrifice to God. This is sometimes marked by a member of the family going to Mecca as the *Hajj* occurs during this month. A lamb may be bought from the *halal* shop and the meat is shared among relatives, neighbours and the poor.

Other causes for celebration are *Moulid* (the Prophet's birthday), New Year and celebrations to mark a pilgrim's return from *Hajj*. Muslim festivals do not happen on the same date each year as the Muslim calendar is lunar. Calendars with both dates are available in Britain.

Discuss

- *How would you explain the meaning of the following to a Muslim: St David's Day, St George's Day, St Andrew's Day, Lent, Pancake Day, Ash Wednesday, Maundy Thursday, Good Friday, Easter Sunday, Ascension, Pentecost, Advent, Christmas? Which is the most important Christian festival do you think?*

Jihad

Jihad means 'striving' and is often translated as 'holy war'. This is not a pillar of Islam, but is considered a religious duty. Often this has been used to justify political or ideological ambition, and sometimes one Muslim nation has declared 'holy war' against another. The term is not always interpreted literally, however; many moderates regard it as an inner struggle against evil, rather than a violent struggle against enemies.

Ritual cleanliness

Pollution by urine, blood or faeces renders a person ritually unclean. Muslim women are ritually unclean during menstruation and after childbirth and are not permitted to touch the Qur'an or perform *namaz*. Ritual cleanliness is also prescribed in the Old Testament. As Christians therefore, we may be able to understand the religious duties and requirements of Muslims more readily than most secular westerners do. One example is at the workplace. Many employers do not understand religious sensibilities and make no allowances for them. Practising Muslims have specific needs at work; they need to be able to have somewhere to perform *namaz* (prescribed prayers) at lunch time. During *ramzan* (Ramadan, the month of fasting), they will have less energy during the day as they must not take any food or drink, not even water, until sundown. Muslim women need to observe some degree of *purdah* at work.

An inner-city vicar once invited the local *imam* (mosque leader) to observe a church service. 'But are these people clean?' the imam asked. It took a moment or two before the vicar realized he wanted to know whether the members of the congregation had performed ritual ablutions before coming to church.

Discuss

- *Read Luke 18:9–14. How does this relate to i) a devout Muslim who observes all the religious requirements of Islam? ii) an evangelical Christian who, being free in Christ, believes Christians who go to confession or cross themselves, or eat fish on Fridays cannot be true Christians?*

- *Reflect on the story of the woman who had had an issue of blood for twelve years (Mark 5:25–34). Imagine her as a Muslim woman, with her Muslim neighbours crowding round to see what's happening. Try telling the story to a female Muslim friend.*

- *Read Matthew 15:1–20. How would you present Jesus' teaching on inner cleansing to your Muslim friends?*

Rites of passage

From the cradle to the grave a Muslim passes through clearly defined stages in his or her life for which there are clear guidelines in the Qur'an and Sunna. The birth of a child is marked by many customs including speaking the *shahada* into the baby's ear. Seven days later the baby is named. The first growth of a baby's hair is shaved to remove all impurities and a sacrifice may be offered. Baby boys are circumcised and in some countries female circumcision is also practised. (There have been some reports of cases of female circumcision in Britain). Forty days after giving birth a mother is considered ritually clean again.[7] At puberty, the child becomes an adult and girls begin to veil. An engagement may be arranged now (unless it was arranged at birth). Marriage is the next stage, followed by motherhood. Then life goes on! Death, the final certainty in life, presents Muslims in Britain with a challenge since they need an Islamic burial on sacred ground; cremation is not allowed.

Discuss

- *All human societies have rites of passage. What importance do they have in the lives of western Christians, compared to our Muslim friends?*

The 'Evil Eye' and the world of folk Islam

In religious matters, it is usually the women who guard and propagate the faith, and it is also the women who tap the spiritual powers on the family's behalf. Women are more involved in superstitious and occult practices than men, as these practices surround life issues such as childbirth, marriage, death, and also relationships between individuals and families. Much is done to placate the evil *jinn* (spirits) who threaten to influence their lives for good or bad.

One Pakistani woman living in Britain recalls how, as a child, the world of folk Islam affected her family:

★　★　★　★　★

'Some neighbours had a quarrel with us. One day, I looked up at the corner of the sitting room ceiling and saw a small object. I took it down and found it to contain a curse, written on a piece of paper in Urdu with Arabic numbers. It was to the effect that there should be enmity between mother and daughter. I and my mother are Christians, however, so we repudiated the effect of the curse in the name of Jesus and threw away the paper. Ever since, whenever we have felt under oppression, we have prayed the Lord's Prayer and read Psalms 91, 92 and 93 and the oppression has gone.'

★　★　★　★　★

This young woman comments that when she is filled with the Holy Spirit and has shared God's truth with Muslims, they have had a trembling fear.

What might be considered occult practices are an everyday reality for many Muslims all over the world. Belief in *nazr* (the 'evil eye', literally 'the eye of jealousy' in Arabic) is widespread through the Muslim Middle East and Muslim and Hindu Indian subcontinent. An envious person can cause crops to fail, a child to be still born or an envious glance at a beautiful baby can cause it to sicken. People do not give compliments, or say that something is beautiful in case they are accused of giving the 'evil eye'. If this does occur, the object is quickly given to the one who admired it, to protect the owner from the curse. Young women are particularly vulnerable to the 'evil eye', so in some communities they are discouraged from going out and attracting envious looks. Protection is also sought through amulets, the wearing of jewellery and red, black and white clothes. The string on which an amulet is hung is usually black for this reason.

Belief in the 'evil eye' is quite common among Pakistani communities in Britain, especially Mirpuris (an area of the Punjab). There are different strands of Islam; some (such as the *Deobandis*) frown on any kind of superstition and preach against the worship of saints (*pirs*) and shrines. Many Muslims in Britain, however, belong to the *Berelvi* sect of Islam, which sets great store by folklore and the spiritual world. Sometimes people pay Muslim holy men for special verses to be cut up and drunk, to help a barren woman conceive, or to heal a sick child. *Zamzam* water from Mecca is also popular as it is regarded as particularly holy.

It is interesting to compare this with the medieval practice of priests selling 'indulgences' to forgive sins. It is also common for Middle Eastern Christian communities to 'christianise' these beliefs, wearing crosses instead of amulets and reading out Psalms in fear rather than in faith to defeat the power of the 'evil eye'. Is the western common practice of wearing Saint Christophers similar to this? These practices are most common among rural communities which perpetuate handed-down traditions. Those who gain more education may not believe in the practices, but will carry them out for the sake (and respect) of their elders.

Knowing these things helps when we meet our Muslim friends in their homes. At the birth of a child you can avoid saying how lovely the child is by saying: 'Thank God that he gave you this child' (using the Arabic phrase *ma sha'a 'llah* meaning 'what God has brought into being'). It is also worth knowing that the phrase for putting a curse on someone, when translated into English is 'doing something' (*kuch kama* in Urdu). So don't be baffled if someone confides in you that so-and-so has 'done something'. It probably means that they have had a quarrel and each fears the other may have cursed her.

A Christian community worker tells the following account of the widespread belief in *jinn*:

★　★　★　★　★

'I asked Naheeda why she had fallen out with Aisha. She said: "One evening, when I was visiting, I realized that she was looking at me as if she was a man. I realized that she had a *jinn* inside her and I was very frightened. I started to dream about it. One night my boyfriend and I woke up at the same time and discovered that we had just had identical dreams about the *jinn*. We were petrified. We went to see the *maulvi* (Muslim priest) and he told us that Aisha has a male *jinn* living in her and if I don't get married then it will come and live in me. That's why I stopped going there. It's dangerous for you to visit, too." I was astonished, but then I remembered. A few months previously, Naheeda had phoned me at 7.00pm and said "I'm getting married in two hours' time. I want you to come." I thought it was very strange and was unable to attend.

'Coming round from my thoughts, I told Naheeda that although I believe that evil spirits exist, I was not afraid because I believed that God would protect me. Aisha was told as a young girl that she would never have children, so the family never tried to get her married. I have occasionally wondered if she is a lesbian and whether she had made some kind of pass at Naheeda. What shocked me most was that I had no idea how much the belief in *jinn* influences people's lives. Now that I am aware of it, I often hear such stories. What surprises me most is that white girls who marry Pakistanis get caught up in this too and will tell you stories of having been visited by *jinn* or affected by curses. I suppose this is one way in which women feel they can effect some kind of influence over their or others' lives.'

* * * * *

Demon possession is a complex area. Suffice it to say that people from traditional cultures set more store in the spirit world than in the world of reason and logical explanations. Sometimes a person believed to be a demon possessed is in reality suffering from mental illness or depression (as described in Ch. 3).

However, there are cases where psychiatrists draw a blank. One account is given from a Middle Eastern country of a Muslim boy who, on completing his reading of the Qur'an, went berserk. No doctor could help him and the father finally brought him to a Christian woman in a hospital 'because I believe Jesus can heal him'. The woman prayed and fasted until she received power from the Holy Spirit—'I felt electrocuted from heaven'—and she knew the Lord wanted her to command the evil spirit out of the boy in Arabic. She took her Bible with her and prayed in the name of Jesus in Arabic for the spirit to leave him. He screamed and foamed at the mouth, and then fell silent. He had been healed. The father believed in Jesus and the people in the wards crowded round to hear the gospel. They had seen that there is power in the name of Jesus.

For an in-depth study of folk Islam, read Bill Musk's book *The Unseen Face of Islam* (see Appendix). He points out that belief in the supernatural, in the spirit world, the world of dreams and visions is widespread across many parts of the world and that it forms a large part of Muslim practice. It is, of course, not limited to the Muslim world; as we have seen, Hindus and Christians are also involved, and Latin American and African tribal religions are full of such practices and beliefs. The divide is really between the rational, post-Enlightenment northern hemisphere and the folkloric, traditional, spiritually aware southern hemisphere.

Dreams and visions

Is this belief in the supernatural the reason why many Muslims all over the world give their lives to Christ, not through rational proclamation from a western missionary, but through direct revelation from God through dreams and visions? Is this also why the West has seen so little revival and so few conversions?

A Lebanese woman, now living in Britain, with wide experience of working as a Christian in the Muslim world remembers many examples of Muslims giving their lives to Christ having seen a dream or vision. She comments that very little affects Muslims until a dream or revelation comes, unexpectedly. Then they are convinced and are even willing to die afterwards. One Muslim man living in a Muslim country in the Middle East had a dream of Jesus dying on the cross for him. He had never read the gospels or the Bible, only the Qur'an. In the dream, Jesus said to him: 'I died for your sins. Believe in me and you will be saved.' The man was very disturbed by his dream and travelled a long way looking for Christians to interpret the dream to him. He found a Christian family who gave him hospitality and showed him the account of the crucifixion in the four gospels. He was astonished to find in print, in a holy book, exactly what he had seen and heard in his dream and he gave his life to the Lord Jesus Christ.

Because of his apostasy, his wife and children were taken from him as demanded by Muslim law (*shariah*). Yet since God had spoken to him so vividly and directly he stood the persecution. Years later he had started a church and was preaching the gospel to other Muslims. There are now a hundred converts and it is the converts who are doing the converting.

Sometimes, as in the Bible, dreams are not only revelatory, they can also warn.[8] In a Middle Eastern country a Sheikh became a Christian. He and his family were in grave danger as three other Sheikhs planned to kill him. One night, the three Sheikhs all had the same dream. They each heard the Lord telling them: 'Be warned, do not touch my servant.' They were awe-struck, knowing that God had spoken to them and warned them; needless to say they abandoned their plans. God still moves powerfully in people's lives just as he did in biblical times. Muslims are open to the spiritual world. They believe the Qur'an was given to Muhammad through a dream. Are Muslims more open than some Christians to the work of God?

Pray

- *Can you pray for Muslims in Britain to have dreams and visions?*
- *Can you pray for Muslim women living in Britain, known to no one, who have had such dreams and visions and who are afraid to tell their family?*

Islamic view of women

Chauvinist Creation

Dear Earth,
   Here is man.
     Love,
       God.

P.S. Here is woman.

Gordon Bailey

Is this the biblical view of creation? Is it the Qur'anic view?

It is important to recognize that there are probably as many different Muslim interpretations of the position of women in the Qur'an, as there are Christian interpretations of the position of women in the Bible. Pioneer work on gender issues in Islam and Christianity has recently been done by Ida Glaser and Napoleon John in their book *Partners or Prisoners?* (see Appendix). They analyze the whole spectrum of Islamic and Christian apologetics regarding the role of women. Islamic views range from conservative traditional (seeing women as weak, confining them to the home), to moderate (supporting some involvement in public and social life), through to liberal (considering the advance in treatment of women at the time of Muhammad an Islamic basis for feminism). Yes, there are feminist Islamic scholars, both male and female! Many Muslim countries also have vibrant women's movements. Asghar Ali Engineer is an activist in the Muslim women's struggle for equality and he reinterprets key Qur'anic passages on women's rights in his book *The Rights of Women in Islam* (see Appendix).

Muslim women themselves have differing opinions about their status in Islam. The debate about women's roles often sounds like that among Christians; the main argument being that different roles for men and women does not imply they are of unequal value. Many young Muslim women growing up in Britain are emphasizing the freedoms which Islam brought for women in the context of the Arabia of the time. They remind us that women of every religion and culture struggle for equality. They point out the degrading treatment of women as sex objects and domestic violence suffered by women in the West. They also remind us of certain uncomfortable biblical passages with which we have to grapple. So this is not a clear cut issue! See the Appendix for a list of books on these issues.

What does the Qur'an actually say about women?

'And women shall have rights . . . to what is equitable; but men have a degree over them' (Sura 2:228). Modern commentators interpret this to mean women have equal legal rights, but that their economic position is such that men must provide for them.

'Men are the protectors and maintainers of women because God has given the one more (strength) than the other,
and because they support them from their means. Therefore
the righteous women are devoutly obedient, and guard in
(the husband's) absence what God would have them guard.
As to those women on whose part ye fear disloyalty and
ill-conduct, admonish them (first), (next) refuse to share their
beds, (and last) beat them (lightly)' (Sura 4:34).

This oft-quoted verse has caused much controversy in the
debate on the treatment of women. The context of Arabian
society was that women did not work and were totally
economically dependent on men. Regarding the light beat-
ing men may give disobedient wives, this is in the context
that women were treated as second-class citizens in that
society, and as such regularly abused. Some commentators
regard this passage as an attempt to restrain, rather than to
encourage physical violence by a husband towards his wife.
Many modern Muslim women believe that the Qur'an
initially improved the condition of women at the time of the
prophet but later on misapplication or misunderstanding of
the verses has resulted in the mistreatment of women. However, many orthodox Muslim commentators do not agree
with contextualisation, since they emphasize that the Qur'an
is universally applicable in all times.

Several passages indicate that a woman's testimony in
court is worth half that of a man and Sura 4:11 clearly states
that a woman's inheritance is half that of her brother.
Commentators explain that in fact this does not penalize
the woman, since there is a far greater financial burden on
her brother than on her. He has to provide for his own

family and for his mother if she is widowed, and even for his sister if she is widowed or in financial straits.

Other verses seem to emphasize spiritual and social equality. Sura 16:99 says that if a person does right (whether male or female) they will be rewarded. Sura 60:12 allows women (at least in theory) to participate in government, public life (Sura 9:71) and war (Sura 3:195).

How did Muhammad treat his wives?

We saw in chapter five how Islam allows polygamy: 'Marry women of your choice, two, or three or four, but if ye fear that ye shall not be able to deal justly then only one . . .' (Sura 4:3). Some scholars see this as implying the prohibition of polygamy since it is only possible for very rich men to be able to treat each wife the same. Interestingly, Tunisia forbids polygamy in its constitution. Muhammad had many wives but Aisha was his favourite. He loved her dearly and died in her arms. Aisha was by no means a doormat. When wrongly accused of adultery by misogynists, she refused to apologize and spoke her mind to her husband. One month later Muhammad had a revelation which declared her innocence, resulting in a Qur'anic verse against slandering good women.

Other Qur'anic verses and *hadith* describe procedures for marriage and divorce (see Ch. 5). It is also clear that Muslim men are allowed to marry non-Muslim women (who are expected to convert) but Muslim women are not allowed to marry non-Muslim men.

What did Muhammad say about women?

Some *hadith* of the prophet Muhammad remind Muslim men to cherish their wives, such as:

> 'The Prophet said: "O people, your wives have certain rights over you and you have certain rights over them. Treat them well and be kind to them for they are your partners and committed helpers." ' Also: 'The Prophet said: "The best among you is the one who is the best towards his wife."'

One *hadith* quotes Aisha as saying that the Prophet 'served his wife', meaning that he did work for his wife.

However, there are others which seem very harsh. Maulana Ashraf Ali Thanvi refers to the well-known *hadith*: 'The Holy Prophet has said to women that he has seen women in hell in large numbers. The women ask why . . . he replied, "because you habitually curse everything, show ingratitude to your husbands and scowl at the things given by them." '[9] Another tradition says: " 'I have not left any calamity more detrimental to mankind than women." '

How do we as Christians react to the view of woman in Islam? Bob Hitching quotes the well-known *hadith*: 'Those who entrust their affairs to a woman will never know prosperity':

> 'That seems rather a strong statement for anyone to swallow. The Muslim feminist then counters with the fact that A'isha, the youngest bride of the prophet, fought the battle to defend the orthodox faith at the time of the prophet's death. By many Muslim scholars however, this was considered "bid'a", an innovation based on errant behaviour. This may sound familiar to those acquainted with the views

of some Christian fundamentalists. When Deborah was raised up to judge and defend Israel she was, according to many commentators, in "ibid'a", that is, God allowed it to happen as a judgement upon the men because they were not godly and were neglecting their responsibilities. I would suggest that in Islam and Christianity a crucial issue is at stake and that is the basic equality of women within the life and culture of society.'[10]

His challenge is clear: 'Too often missions coming from a conservative perspective breed a male dominated world-view which fits quite well into a Muslim paradigm. There is much to suggest that a new Christian theology of the role of women may well be overdue in the modern world.'[11]

Theology is one thing; practice is another. We can interpret, reinterpret and contextualise Qur'anic verses and prophetic traditions on this subject for ever, but this is secondary to how Muslim women's lives are affected in practice. We need to ask our Muslim friends how they themselves feel about their status in Islam and be prepared to be surprised by their answers!

Politics, citizenship and Muslim culture

In a way which is hard for western Christians to understand, Muslim culture, politics and religion are inextricably linked. Islam is not simply a set of beliefs, a pattern of religious practices and traditions or a code of moral behaviour and human virtues; instead it is a whole way of life, an economic, social and political system regulating the behaviour and relationships of its members through its own civil and criminal law. It forms the particular world-view of its members and gives guidance for life in this world and the next. Western Christians, on the other hand, tend to separate out their faith, culture, political affiliation and national identity. We may even deny we have a culture, because: 'in Christ there is no East and West' and 'my life is now hidden in Christ'. Yet are we really that culture-less? Ch. 8 explores Christianity and culture in more detail.

Every Muslim belongs to the world-wide body of believers (*ummah*). The word *ummah* occurs sixty-four times in the Qur'an[12] and is usually translated 'Muslim community'. It denotes a people to whom God sends a prophet, or who are objects of his plan of salvation and it expresses the essential unity of Muslims in diverse cultural settings. After the death of the prophet, the period of the *Khalif* (caliph) established the link between the solidarity of the Muslim community and political power. This resulted in the rule of Arab dynasties which lasted for many years. In the twentieth century the term came to mean the nation-state. Nowadays, loyalty to Islam is emphasized, rather than race, language or geography.

Reflect

- *How does the sense of bonding, strength and encouragement embodied by the ummah compare with the world-wide Body of Christ? - Is our identity as members of this Body stronger than our local or ethnic identity?*

One obstacle to world-wide Islamic unity, however, is that very soon after the prophet's death, the movement split into two main camps which still exist today: Shia and Sunni. Ninety per cent of the world's Muslims are Sunni; only ten per cent are Shi'ites, living in Iran, Iraq, Lebanon and scattered in Turkey and the West. The Shi'ites follow only those descended from Muhammad's cousin Ali, whereas the Sunnis follow the line of Caliphs who had been Muhammad's 'Companions'.

The Qur'an and *hadith* provide the laws and rules by which the *ummah* must live. In some countries there is strict shariah law, such as in Saudi Arabia, where Qur'anic laws are interpreted strictly; strict separation of the sexes is enforced, thieves' hands are cut off and no alcohol is allowed. However, many other Muslim countries have various systems of government, including kings, presidents, military rule and family dynasties. Political parties are also part of the present day scene.

The question arises: what is the link between religion and citizenship? Here are some snippets of conversations between Jane, an English Christian and some young Asian girls:

Jane:	'What religion is Nahim?'
Rifat:	'He's Bengali.'
Jane:	'Is Shibli Bengali?'
Rifat:	'Yes, she's a Muslim.'
Gulshan:	'Shaheen is not really Asian.'
Jane:	'Why not?'
Gulshan:	'She's a Christian.'

However, the Qur'an assumes the existence of a Muslim state. This presents Muslims in Britain with a dilemma since they are a religious minority in a non-Muslim state. How is it possible then to follow the Qur'an, when the laws of the country they live in are not Muslim ones and when their religious and national identities are not one and the same?

Reflect

- As Christians, do we ever find the laws of the state conflict with our Christian beliefs? What is our response? How similar or different is this from the situation for Muslims when their beliefs conflict with the state's laws?

- Reflect on the Christian view of citizenship. What was Jesus' teaching on this? What is the difference between Islam as a political system, as laid out in the Qur'an, and the socio-political status of Christianity implied in the Bible?

- Reflect on political and social minorities and the powerless in the Bible (the theology of 'the remnant'). What does this demonstrate in contrast to Islam?

The second issue is that to stop believing in Islam is to be charged with treason. Christian converts in a Muslim country lose their citizenship (and may lose their lives). Here in Britain converts do not commit treason against their country, but they are accused of betraying their loyalty to family, community and *ummah*.

British Muslims' involvement in civic life

As outlined in Ch. 1, Muslim communities in Britain are in no way homogeneous. When the majority community asks for a spokesperson from 'the Asian community', it is like asking for one person in Europe to speak on behalf of all! Muslims are put in an impossible situation when they are asked to provide one person as a representative, as we saw in Ch. 3 with regard to the SACRE. Often, the white community's demand for the 'view' of Muslims on complex issues means that the most vocal and sophisticated put themselves forward as spokesmen of the community, whether or not they have the support of that community. This means that probably the vast majority are not able to express their opinions.

And finally . . . Islam on the move?

It cannot be denied that Islam is 'on the move' across Africa and Europe; it is, like Christianity, a missionary religion and seeks converts. In Muslim countries anyone who is born a Muslim and leaves the faith is guilty of the grave sin of apostasy and as such may be killed. Evil and cruelty has been (and in some countries is still being) perpetrated in the name of triumphant Islam. History shows that in the hands of evil men, religious fervour can be put to evil purposes. Muslim fanatics and student zealots are gaining ground. Revivalist Muslim movements are increasing in Britain too and universities are a hotbed of Muslim/Christian debate. So in these days of resurgent, militant Islam what is the most legitimate Christian response? Is it right to meet threat with fear or counter threat?

If anyone has been to villages in the Indian subcontinent they must have seen the mosque facades. The front wall is strong, beautiful and impressive, but it is just a facade. There is nothing behind it, only an empty courtyard. Is this a symbol for Islam itself? Muslim speakers at Hyde Park Corner or in Muslim/Christian debates become very heated and sometimes express their anger violently. But does God need defending? Then again, could the loud posturing of Muslims in the Rushdie affair have been a smoke screen for the insecurity of youths who, feeling marginalised in British society, hanker after a strong Muslim identity? As one youth who took part in the Bradford book-burning told me: 'I wasn't doing it for Allah. I don't really know much about my religion. I was doing it to defend myself. I'm not accepted as British, so I have to defend my religion. It's the only part of my identity which no-one can take from me.'

Discuss

- *What is your response when Christians say Islam is completely of the devil or that there is no such thing as 'moderate Islam'? How do you respond to those who say it is a good religion and we can find God through it?*

- *'I've never met "Islam"; I've only met Muslims.' Canon Dr Philip Lewis, Bradford. What is the point he is making and do you agree?*

Notes

1. There are also many 'unorthodox' groups and sects within Islam.
2. Suzanne Haneef, *What everybody should know about Islam*, p. 25.
3. Muslims and Christians disagree about the status of Muhammad as the last prophet. Sura 61:6 of the Qur'an suggests that Muhammad was predicted in the New Testament: 'Jesus . . . giving glad tidings of an apostle to come after me, whose name shall be Ahmad.'
4. John 1:18, Ephesians 1:3–4, John 17:2–9, John 1:1 and 14, John 14:16–17.
5. The recorded sayings/traditions of Muhammad.
6. The leaflet *True Fasting* produced in English and Urdu, is a useful resource, produced by WORD OF LIFE (see Appendix).
7. Did you know the Anglican church used to conduct a service called 'The Churching of Women' forty days after giving birth?
8. See Genesis 20:3, Genesis 31:24 and Psalm 105:15.
9. Maulana Ashraf Ali Thanvi, *Bashishti Zewar (Heavenly Ornaments)*, p. 474.
10. Bob Hitching, *McDonalds, Minarets and Modernity*, p. 66.
11. *Ibid.*, p. 45.
12. Qur'anic references include: Sura 6:42, 10:47, 13:30, 16:34, 10:9, 3:110, 4:41.

Part III

Christianity and Islam

Outreach and the Church

'The Church is the only institution which exists for the benefit of the outsider.'
William Temple

We've all seen it: the redundant inner-city church, now a carpet warehouse or a library, maybe even a mosque. 'Times have changed,' sigh those who were baptised there seventy years ago, 'and not for the better. These foreign religions are taking over.'

Some churches in Asian areas struggle on with a handful of members, for whom Sunday mornings provide a welcome haven of English culture. Many feel threatened by a culture they do not understand, and the farthest thing from their minds is the idea that they should actually befriend their Muslim neighbour! Yet this is exactly where opportunities for bridge-building and faith-sharing are at their greatest. It is also the calling of the church.

Those who have the vision are often frustrated that some who support mission overseas or Christian Aid ignore the needs of their Asian next-door neighbour. Many Christians simply do not believe that Muslims can or need to be reached with the gospel, and do not realize how spiritually hungry many Muslims actually are. So how do those who have the vision motivate the church? One key is to start where the churches actually are, not where we would like them to be! Most churches in both suburban areas and inner cities have a whole variety of different views about their Asian neighbours; cultural and 'nationalistic' views often get confused with religious and witnessing issues, so a great deal of digging beneath the surface of what people say is required.

Take the statement: 'I think Asians should follow our ways, after all this is a Christian country, so they shouldn't be allowed their mosques'. But what are 'our ways'? Muslim families living in the inner city may think our ways are miniskirts and vandalism. And what do you think about mosques? In fact, most mosques are built with private, not council funds and provide a safe meeting place for Muslims to fulfil their religious obligations.

Why reach out?

Remember (in Ch. 2) Jackie Pullinger's reminder that God says 'Go!' (Matthew 28:18–20)? Actually, in the Greek, the emphasis is on the verb 'make disciples' rather than on going. Jesus' words are quite clear. He gives the justification for mission: 'All authority in heaven and on earth has been given to me' and follows it with the command: 'Therefore go and make disciples of all nations . . .'

There is, however, in the churches a whole spectrum of attitudes towards Muslims (and other faiths). Some Christians do not affirm Muslim culture because they disagree with Islam (or resent the presence of Asians in their area) and want to convert Muslims to Christianity; perhaps also to their own brand of western culture? Other Christians are exactly the opposite; they contrast the decay of western society with the positives in Islamic culture and faith and see no need for evangelism. Other Christians respect Muslims and affirm the positives in their faith and culture, but want to share with them the forgiveness, salvation, joy and peace of Christ. Muslims find nothing strange in this; they may also want to convert their Christian friends to Islam!

The gospel of Christ: good news for Muslim women

'He loves us, and by his sacrificial death he has freed us from our sins.'[1]

This is Good News! It is easy to get bogged down in theological complications when talking with Muslims, but the central message of the love and saving power of God through Jesus Christ is amazingly simple, yet so hard for Muslims to grasp. Can you think of anything humanity needs more to know than that God loves us and has freed us from our sins?

A Muslim woman in a Middle Eastern country who became a follower of Christ said: 'It was the love of Muhammad (a convert to Christianity) which made me understand the love of Jesus. I had never seen it in Muslim men before.' So many others have a similar testimony: 'It was not what they said which convinced me, it was their love.'

Many also testify that they have come to know Jesus as their Lord and Saviour through suffering. The paradox of the suffering God is anathema to orthodox Islam. God is great; he cannot be weak and suffer. Yet suffering is at the very heart of human existence and it is the literal 'crux' of the Christian gospel. It is through God's suffering that he saves us and that death is defeated. The challenge is to us to follow Christ in the way of the Cross as we witness to our Muslim friends. Vivienne Stacey urges Christians to follow this way: 'In these days of resurgent Islam, Christians have a unique opportunity to respond, not with counter-moves or rival programmes, but with the love which suffers and endures. Christ . . . deliberately chose the way of the Cross. As his followers, so must we. Out of our weakness God will show his strength.'[2]

Ch. 11 'The Suffering God' gives a biblical reflection on the salvation which the suffering Christ has to offer our Muslim women friends.

Doubts and dilemmas

Evangelical Christians have no problem with the intellectual concept of reaching out with the gospel to our friends and family, whether they have a faith or none. Yet the practical outworking of this is often far more complex than the idea. In getting to know Muslim women as friends, our understanding of our own faith may be challenged, or deepened and our understanding of their faith may also be challenged or deepened. You may like to reflect on the following story by a former church lay worker among Muslim women. It is an honest account of the doubts and dilemmas we may face when we actually engage in sharing deeply with Muslim friends:

★ ★ ★ ★ ★

A story of a friendship

'She came from a small village in Pakistan, brought over to this town to marry her cousin. She was only sixteen, could not speak any English and had had no education. I first met her when she came to an English class with her mother-in-law shortly after her arrival.

'There is a sadness in her life. What can I offer her? Could I share with her what I believe? Have I any right to tell someone more devout than I shall ever be, that my 'religion' is the one she should be following? She once told me: "I love God and my religion; I look forward to my fast, it brings me so close to my God and it makes me feel fit and well." There was excitement in her voice as she spoke. She always prays five times a day; if I unthinkingly call at prayer time, it does not matter to her, she will still kneel in the corner of the room and pray. Once I called and she was more welcoming than usual: "Oh, I've been praying for you today, and here you are." Dear Lord, do you really answer their prayers too? Forgive me for limiting you.

'Sometimes, wearied with family problems and disputes, she has black circles under her eyes through lack of sleep.

"You must get a good night's sleep", I tell her. Yet I know that she will have been up at 5 or 6 o'clock every morning for her first prayer, nothing would make her miss that. Dear Lord, how often have I gone for days without speaking to you?

'Another visit and more family problems; she was very tearful, again not sleeping well, but God was helping her, she told me, and she was trusting him; she would make sure that she was going to do the right thing in this particular situation, for there were two angels watching over her actions, one noting down all the good things she does, one all the bad, ready for the day of reckoning. My mind went to Matthew 25, the sheep and the goats. Was it the same? I felt confused. Was this the moment to share the gospel with her, or would that upset her even more? I let the moment pass; perhaps another time . . .

'We have many chats about religion. She believed when she came to Britain that all white people were Christians, and was surprised when I told her the true situation. Another time we talked about the things we have in common; our relationship with God, although she seems to fear him more than I, how we should obey him and be good to others, and so on. I thought of the number of times that people have asked me: "Have you any converts yet?" If I 'converted' my dear friend, she would be banished from the family, ostracized, an outcast. The family in Pakistan would be affected too.

Go then to all people everywhere and make them disciples . . .
Dear Lord, what am I to do?'

★ ★ ★ ★ ★

Discuss

- *Consider the biblical basis for mission.*
- *Have you been challenged similarly by the faith of a Muslim friend? How have you responded to the challenge?*
- *Discuss the question: 'Dear Lord, what am I to do?' Make a note to come back to this story and compare it with 'Counting the Cost' in Ch. 10.*

Encouraging the church to reach out

How can you, your church, or a group within your church be encouraged to reach out to Muslim friends and neighbours? Here are some ideas.

Get together and pray

Most churches do not have special outreach to Asians, nor prayer support groups, although reaching Asians may be included in their evangelistic programmes. There are, however, inter-church support groups for Christians up and down the country. One such group is the South Manchester Muslim Support Group, with members from five churches in South Manchester, who want to get to know their Muslim neighbours and learn how to share the gospel with them. There are around twelve members and they meet once a month on Sunday afternoons for prayer and the sharing of experiences.

Anne Cooper[3] is a founding member of the group and comments:

'It has seemed that we are at two stages. Firstly, there are those who have Muslim neighbours and who have reacted in a negative way to their differing customs, but now want to learn to understand and relate more closely. Secondly, there are those who already have Muslim friends and want to move from a purely social relationship to being able to share their faith together.'

There are many pressures we may feel when we get involved in Muslim women's lives; we may find it hard to switch off from the burden of friends' difficult situations; in becoming friends and even 'sisters' we have demands and duties to fulfil; we may feel we ourselves are living in two cultures, not fully understood by either; fellow Christians may express unacknowledged racist feelings to us; single women may become over-involved and be under-supported. Are we supported by our church leaders, or do they regard sipping tea with Muslim women as less important than debating with male mosque leaders?

All this means that prayer support from those who know us and care about us is essential. Can you get others to come along with you from the church when you visit your friends? That is often the only way to get the message across that this is a long-term ministry, with lots of encouragements, but also often disappointments. We may not see any results at all, but this is another cultural adjustment western, goal- and results-oriented Christians need to make!

From little acorns . . .

When we start to pray, things start to happen. In 1995 local Christians from various churches in a town in the South of England joined together to pray because of a common concern for outreach to their Muslim neighbours. As a result of this prayer, a young woman was called to Christian work in the area. She in turn prayed that a Christian family would move into an estate where there were several Asian families. The following week it was discovered that a family from another church had just done that. In another part of the town, a Christian woman came to teach in a 98 per cent Asian school, and several other Christian couples all felt called to move into the area. 'The impact of the church united is fundamental,' comments the new worker. 'We are presenting Jesus, not our own denominations, and we are allowing the Holy Spirit to do the work.'

Become informed

By 1996 thirty-five people from several different local churches in the area had joined a course on reaching out to Muslims. At one of the course sessions, a health visitor and a doctor's receptionist had quite a surprise. Not only were they unaware the other was a Christian, but they were also amazed to discover that they had both had contact with the same Muslim family and had been able to share Jesus with them during a difficult time. The health visitor commented: 'I thought I was on my own in this.

We are individual pebbles and we need each other.'

In some cities churches employ advisors on multifaith issues, as well as lay workers in community or race relations. These workers hold seminars for churches, raising awareness of multifaith issues and encouraging churches to get involved in bridge-building and faith sharing. These seminars do not need to be high-powered or terribly intellectual. People do not need to know the Qur'an inside out to be able to make friends with Muslim women, but it is good to know the basics of Islamic beliefs, as outlined in Ch. 7. The key is to see where the churches are and what they want. Some churches have Asian evenings, with quizzes, Asian food, a video or perhaps a talk by an Asian Christian. Some hold racism awareness days and seminars, or follow study courses. Sometimes information about reaching out to Asian neighbours can be integrated into a course already in existence, such as a Lent course, evangelism course or a house group programme. The Appendix has details of many courses and study aids available for churches. Many areas have locally devised courses.[4]

Other members of your church may be quite happy for you to reach out to Muslims but personally, it's not their 'thing'. It's true that not everyone may be called but everyone needs to be informed. What happens if a Muslim comes to church? The implications are far-reaching for the whole church as the Body of Christ. Ch. 10 explores this in more detail.

Discuss

- *Can you form a church prayer group to pray for Muslim friends and colleagues, and for those who are building friendships with them?*
- *Can you get your minister to read this book?*
- *Can you or your minister find out what training resources exist in your area? Will your minister incorporate one of them into the church's programme?*

Join in a Christian community project

For several years there has been an increasing realization that churches of all denominations need to be at the forefront of providing care and service to the local community outside the church, not just to the members of the church. The advantage for Christians in working in church-based projects is that there is the freedom to share one's faith where appropriate. Such projects, however, are often strapped for cash, as many long-term funding opportunities from secular sources may be forfeited.

It is an irony that the need for such projects is greatest in inner-city areas where churches are at their weakest, resources are at their lowest, and long-term funding needs are at their greatest. The Church Urban Fund was set up by the Church of England in response to the report *Faith in the City* (1985) and other projects have been set up in the '90s, such as UK Action (Tear Fund and Evangelical Alliance). Another way is for wealthier suburban churches to catch the vision for mission in the inner city and go into partnership with inner-city churches and their projects. Sometimes, churches find it easier to support those who go thousands of miles abroad to 'do mission', whilst two miles down the road there are pioneering mission projects, struggling to survive.

Suggestion

- *If your church is concerned about outreach but you have no Muslim neighbours, can you 'go into partnership' with an inner-city church which has? (Or vice versa!)*

What kind of projects?

Bassi Mirzania, Director of Social Responsibility for the Diocese of Guildford, has several suggestions for church outreach projects. As well as language classes, befriending schemes, mother and toddler groups, advice centres and refuges, she goes on to note: 'A professional legal advice and translation of documents office could be set up. Maybe the need will arise for battered women or pregnant girls to be taken into the homes of believers.' With regard to language classes she comments: 'We need to be sensitively aware of Muslim women's cultural expectations and make sure there are no men in the building, for example, and that the teachers are female. If this is a problem, then teaching English on a one-to-one basis either in their home or ours would be preferable. We need to be professional, impartial and non-racist.'

Bassi also advocates an open attitude towards Muslims in the neighbourhood: 'One church I know has recently allowed the church hall to be used by the Muslim community for morning prayer meetings. This has been a courageous step for them and they are to be commended for not feeling threatened. It is the first step towards communicating positively with the Muslim community.' Bassi has another imaginative suggestion for opening up two-way lines of communication: 'Intellectual Muslim women would love to be invited to local lectures in your area, and even to be asked to give talks on their lives and experiences to groups within the church. Why should they always listen to us?'

The co-ordinator of a church-based drop-in centre for Asians has one phrase which sums up church-based community work among Muslims: 'sticking with it'. 'For the first two years of my job, I hated it,' she admits, 'but I stuck with it, and I am now amazed at how it has developed.' She says there is no point in going into short-term projects: 'When we opened our drop-in centre, the first question Asian people asked was' "how long are you going to stay here?" They are used to short-term projects setting up, ticking the "Equal Opportunities" box and then going away again.'

This account by a community worker in Scotland is an example of the situations she and her team of volunteers meet on a day to day basis:

* * * * *

'Khalida wheeled her baby's buggy through the office door, sat down on the sofa and burst into tears. Constantly on the receiving end of her alcoholic father's outbursts and forced to be the family skivvy, she had had enough; she wanted to leave home. Her husband was in India and likely to remain there as their marriage had not been a good match. It took many months of negotiations with the local council before she was allocated a house, in which time we visited her and made trips together to various offices. This would be her first experience of living alone.

'Just as she was about to move, Khalida's baby was taken very seriously ill and had to be hospitalised. Her relations came only briefly to see her and the child; we visited as we could. One day she asked who paid us to do our work. I said I was paid by the church but that everyone else worked for free; she could not believe this. She asked us to pray for her child's recovery.

'When she finally got into her new house, Christian volunteers visited regularly to see how she was getting on. I popped in one day and she asked "What is a church?" I talked about the fact that we do our work because Jesus asked us to love our neighbours as we love ourselves. She was amazed to discover that we had been praying for her and her baby in our morning prayers. "You believe in Jesus just like we believe in Muhammad, don't you?" she said. I replied that it wasn't quite the same. "You believe he's God's son, don't you?" "That's right." "He was hanged, wasn't he?" I was then able to explain why Jesus died on the cross for us all. We got into a discussion then about holy books and she brought out her Qur'an for me to see. I was very aware that while she would hardly be called a devout Muslim, Khalida had covered her walls in Qur'anic verses and magic numbers. She is still very insecure about living alone.

'I don't know where all this will lead with Khalida. Her curiosity has obviously been aroused by the love she has experienced from the Christian friends she has made. It is tempting to want to start pushing conversations about Jesus when an interest has been expressed but I believe we should go at Khalida's speed. After all, at the end of the day, it is about the Holy Spirit working in her, rather than our efforts. We will continue to pray for her, support her and take opportunities to share with her.'

* * * * *

Discuss

- *Can you find out whether there are Christian workers among Muslims in your area and support them? - Can you join as a volunteer?*
- *What role do you think the church has, or should have, in a multifaith area?*
- *How can Christian community work become more relevant to Muslim women?*
- *How can long-term projects be set up, with adequate funding and sound management structures?*
- *How can we envision funding agencies and suburban churches to reach out to inner-city Muslim women?*

A cautionary note: The lure of the West?

Occasionally a Muslim woman or girl may appear to embrace Christianity, when in fact she is embracing liberated western values. A Christian community worker came across the following situation which illustrates the confusion in the minds of both Christian workers and Asian girls between Christian and western culture:

* * * * *

Girls from a variety of Asian backgrounds attended a young women's discussion group run on church premises. There was a variety of activities and no apology was made for having a 'God-slot'. It was a safe female environment and parents seemed to be happy that the girls were attending this rather than a secular group. Perhaps, though, the girls saw it differently. Many of the leaders were single Christian women living independent lives. It was a chance to get away from home for a few hours, to discuss fashion, boys and other subjects parents frown on.

Sonia, a sweet, quiet Muslim girl, joined the group. She appeared quite 'interested in the gospel' and for a time attended one-to-one Bible studies. Sonia left school with poor qualifications, but found her way onto a college course and worked very hard. One of the leaders would visit and help her with her homework, being made very welcome by the family. Sonia opened up to the leader and shared her worries. On the surface she obeyed her parents. She wore western clothes which broadly conformed to the Muslim dress code, although she did not cover her head. Although she never went to wild parties and was usually home before dark, she may have had a secret boyfriend. Eventually she got a job and then voluntarily and happily entered into an arranged marriage.

The leader reflected subsequently on her friendship with Sonia. In retrospect, Sonia's interest in Christianity seemed superficial. She had never made any pretence of becoming a Christian. Had she just wanted the friendship of the leaders? Was religion just a passing phase?

* * * * *

Refer back to 'Issues for teenage girls' in Ch. 5.

Discuss

- *A Muslim girl tells you her parents are cruel, not allowing her to see any boys, and ignorant: 'My mum can't even speak English.' She asks you to give her a lift to see her boyfriend. What is going on inside her when she says this? - What 'stage' is she going through? - Why do you think she has chosen you (a non-Asian) to say this to? - How will you respond?*

- *Do you think she would have said this to an Asian Christian?*

Imagine your church is considering doing youth work among young Muslim women.

Discuss the following questions:

- *Will the Christian emphasis of the group be stated?*
- *To what extent is the work going to be evangelistic?*

- *Is there value in having a work which does not attempt to evangelize at all?*
- *Where will the activities take place, in someone's home or in a church?*
- *Who will the helpers be: Christians, non-Christians, Asian, English?*
- *How old will they be and what marital status? What style of clothing will they wear?*
- *Will they meet with the approval of the girls' parents? What contact will the leaders have with the parents?*
- *Will the leaders encourage girls to respect their parents' values (which ones?) or will they promote western values (which ones?)*

The section 'Faith at fifteen' in Ch. 10 explores the issues youth groups may face if a girl professes faith in Christ.

Dig deep: can we distinguish faith and culture?

Remember (in Ch. 7) the snippets of conversations between Jane, an English Christian and some young Asian girls? Let's look again at the conversation between Jane and Gulshan. Gulshan is a Pakistani teenager from a Muslim family; she and her friend Shaheen have recently made a commitment to Christ:

Gulshan: 'Shaheen is not really Asian.'
Jane: 'Why not?'
Gulshan: 'She's a Christian.'

As we have seen, nationality, religion and culture are all inextricably linked in Islam. Though this is not the case in Christianity, many Muslims see the Christian faith as 'the white man's religion'.

Discuss

- *What is going on in Gulshan's mind as she equates being Christian with being non-Asian?*

- *What part do you think the church she and Shaheen go to may have unwittingly played in this? (they are the only non-white members).*

- *In your church how many times do non-western Christians lead church services, preach, teach and share faith insights from a non-western perspective? How many times have they been invited to do so?*

- *How can we mirror Christian biblical culture in our churches?*

Discuss the following examples of religious practices. Are they cultural or biblical?:

- *Men and women sitting together in church.*

- *Women covering their heads for worship and prayer.*

- *Greeting one another with a kiss, hug or handshake.*

- *The meeting should start and finish on time so as to be 'orderly' (1 Corinthians 14:40).*

- *Drinking wine at the Lord's supper.*

- *Church leadership is for males only.*

- *Saying grace before meals.*

Back to our snippets of conversation. Shibli, a Bangladeshi teenager, has just visited Bangladesh for the first time. On her return she reports: 'I am so excited because I have found lots of Bengali Christians and churches. I never knew they existed in our country.' A young Pakistani woman who came to faith in Christ in this country found the same exhilaration and sense of belonging when she visited Pakistan and found other Pakistani Christians worshipping in Punjabi, having a totally Pakistani culture and identity as Pakistani Christians. This is something she still yearns for in Britain.

Get multicultural!

According to the Alliance of Asian Christians, there are an estimated 40–45,000 Asian Christians in Britain. Asian Christian Fellowships are growing and thriving in the UK and are a vital part of the Christian life of Britain. Many Asian Christians worship in mainstream churches on a Sunday morning and also meet in Asian Christian fellowships in the afternoon; some fellowships are churches in their own rights. In many cases, Asian Christians from a variety of backgrounds attend and several different languages are spoken.

Often the best witnesses to Muslims are Asian Christians as they have a common cultural heritage and demonstrate the fact that Christianity is not just for white people. For converts and Muslim enquirers, Asian Christian fellowships are a useful half-way house. New converts may feel much more comfortable in an Asian cultural context than in a mainly white church as they explore their new- found faith. Asian Christians can be a vital model for new Christians to affirm their Asian roots. Some new believers may not feel an Asian fellowship is appropriate for them, especially if they are already very westernized or the church is multicultural. In all of this, there can be no generalizations. Everyone has different needs.

Christians from Asian backgrounds are also invaluable to the mainstream white churches, both in helping them appreciate Asian culture and in encouraging them to believe that God is able to save Muslims (and Hindus, Sikhs and Buddhists). If your church asks a white person to 'talk about the Asian communities', why not suggest instead that an Asian Christian, or even a Muslim person should be invited instead?

Let's hear from Shuguftah, a British Asian woman who came to faith in Christ. What does she want to say to the mainly white church in Britain about reaching out to Muslims?

* * * * *

'There's no ABC guide. Ultimately we're all individuals. We all have a distinct family and background. It's very easy to lump people together, saying "They're Pakistani, so they must be like this, or they're English so they must be like this". My family and I are all individuals.

'Question your own understanding of other religions. Encourage others to question their own religion. Use dialogue. The first point isn't to tell people about Jesus. It is to allow them to discover for themselves that where they are isn't the right place.

'Don't be afraid. Most Asian people are very friendly and hospitable. Don't be patronizing. Be genuine. People can see through you when you're just wanting to get to the "Jesus bit". Your actions speak louder than your words. You may never have to speak about Jesus. It may be just through your actions that the Lord will bring them to himself, such as sharing your possessions, inviting people for meals, or a cup of tea. The Asian community shares their money, possessions and children. If you want to witness you have to become part of the community.

'It is important to realize that Christianity is multicultural. It is not a white man's religion. Jesus was not white, he was brown. Present Christianity as a multicultural religion. Take your Asian friend to an Asian Christian Fellowship meeting first, rather than them going to a church with hundreds of white faces. Give him or her a New Testament in their mother tongue. There is still the assumption that if you're brown you go to a mosque and if you're white you go to church. We all have a bit of power in changing that. We are the church; our little bit is vital.

'Open the lines of communication. Actively listen to what Asian people have to say about how they feel about being a minority, about their religion, about their family, about racism, about politics. Don't be scared to give your telephone number, or to drop in. Take risks.

'Above all, be genuine, have faith and pray. It does work. Because someone, somewhere along the line took a risk to speak to me about Christ.'

* * * * *

Find Out

- *Are there Asian Christians you know, or are you an Asian Christian who would be available to share with Anglo Christians from an Asian perspective?*

- *Find out about courses put on by Asian Christian organisations (see Appendix).*

How not to hide Jesus

The above suggestions give you ways of getting this issue onto your church's agenda. So far, so good. But what about actually sharing the gospel with Muslims? Here are a few pointers.

Theology

In a conversation about our faith, we may know what we mean, but how is it understood by the other? As we saw in Ch. 7, Muslims think that Christians believe in three gods, so it is best to avoid starting a conversation with 'I believe that Jesus is the Son of God'. Asian Christians and Muslim converts are of key importance in helping non-Asian Christians understand the way Muslims think about God. Word of Life's Bible Correspondence course is an excellent resource in this respect, as are their leaflets on aspects of the Christian faith, available in English or Urdu (see Appendix).

In the West Midlands, Pall Singh has initiated an adaptation of the nationwide *Alpha* course, looking at Christianity from an Asian point of view. Rather than starting with 'Who is Jesus?', the first topic is prayer. Other Asian-friendly questions are 'How can we resist evil?' These are natural topics for Asians who, unlike most westerners already have the foundation of a belief in God. The course is aimed at British Asians who want to know 'How can this be applied to me as an Asian?', 'Can I keep my Asian culture?' 'What about marriage?' This practical approach to 'theology' is particularly important when reaching out to Muslim women for whom conversion is likely to affect all aspects of life.[5]

Gifts of the Holy Spirit

Anne Cooper points out: 'Mission to Muslims is not necessarily so much a matter of trying to convey critical information, against most of which the Muslim is already "inoculated". It is a question of preaching the gospel with power, with the Holy Spirit, and with deep conviction, as well as with words (1 Thessalonians 1:5).'[6]

As we saw in Ch. 7 it is important to understand the Islamic world-view, where God is ever present and to be revered, and where supernatural beings, dreams and visions are taken seriously. Do we as Christians need to believe more in the power of God in our everyday lives and witness? Do we need to believe that the gifts of the Holy Spirit are there for us as powerful signs of his presence in our lives? Many believe that this is the key to sharing the gospel with Muslim women in this country who are longing to see God work powerfully in their lives.

One young woman recounts how she was asked to pray for healing for a Muslim friend:

* * * * *

'After an English lesson and meal, I was relaxing with five Muslim children and their mother in the lounge. Then their mother lay on the floor on her back. I asked her what was wrong, and, by using the children to translate, she explained she had backache, and asked if I would pray for her. I said "Yes, I will. I'll pray for you tonight." I didn't exactly spend ages praying about it, but when I went back the next day she told me her back was better! One of the children asked if I'd prayed, and when I said "yes", they were very excited and saw it as an answer to prayer. Since then the mother has asked me to pray for her eyesight . . . and her driving test!'

★ ★ ★ ★ ★

Reflect

- *Reflect whether the Lord is asking you to pray for healing for your Muslim friends.*

Appropriate communication

As we saw in the section 'Tell me a story' in Ch. 4, Asian culture is closer than western culture to Scripture in its circular thought processes and love of storytelling. Doesn't the wind of the Holy Spirit often blow 'all over the place' (my paraphrase of John 3:8)? Isn't telling stories, parables and proverbs therefore a more culturally appropriate and Jesus-like method of sharing the truths of Christ with our Muslim friends than linear, 'theo-logical' debate? Many would say a resounding 'yes!'

Vivienne Stacey tells in her excellent booklet *Practical Lessons for Evangelism among Muslims* how one of her Pakistani friends jokingly chided her: 'You westerners, you leave nothing to the imagination!'[7] Vivienne obviously rose to the challenge, as a few pages later she tells how one day she used her imagination to give out gospels on a bus in Pakistan. Most of the other passengers were farmers. One asked another what he had in his bag. He replied he had carrots. How do you think Vivienne turned this into an opportunity for sharing the gospel?[8]

Stories about human patience, love or hope can also be used to illustrate characteristics of God. A friend told me how she used a story by Adrian Plass to illustrate how we need to give our heart to God (see Matthew 6:19–21).[9] She found the story was a springboard for sharing the gospel with a thirteen-year-old Muslim girl: 'When we got to the end, my friend started asking me questions about Jesus, and her eight-year-old brother, who had come in part-way through, joined in. They said they believed in God. I said I did too, but that Jesus was my friend and he helped me get to know God better and show me what God was like. They then started asking about what happened to Jesus on the cross, and they seemed shocked and sorry for him. That was as far as we got, but I certainly hope to use some more stories soon.'

Storytelling, singing, parables, proverbs and poems are particularly appropriate in the instinctive world of women and the imaginative world of children. One day I visited a family who were going through a hard time. I wanted to communicate the peace of the Lord Jesus and the joy of his salvation. Yet my Punjabi and the mother's English were both insufficient for the task. I remembered an Urdu Christian praise song sung in Asian Christian fellowships, called *Khushi, Khushi Manao* (Rejoice, rejoice!).[10] The song tells how Jesus came to save us, how he suffered on the cross and died, but rose again; he's now our Lord. Let's praise his name! The mother perked up and joined in, singing the words and tapping her foot to the joyful tune. She kept singing it to herself long after I'd stopped singing. I was amazed that this strict Muslim was singing about the salvation of Jesus! A thousand theological discussions with her about the cross of

Christ could not have conveyed the message as effectively as this song did. Singing a song is, of course, a million miles away from trusting her life to the Lord Jesus (and could I imagine her ever coming to church?), yet a seed may have been sown in her heart.

I also remember visiting a Muslim family one day, just as the eight-year-old son came home from school. 'Auntie,' he said, shyly, 'do you think Jesus really did feed five thousand people?' 'Yes, I do,' I said, to which he confidently replied, 'I do too. I like Jesus. He's nice.' Had he been given information about the kindness of Jesus, to which he had given his intellectual assent? No, instead he had heard the story and imagined himself as one of the five thousand hungry people. How hungry he was, and how wonderful of Jesus to give him a nice fresh fish and hunk of bread to tuck into. Jesus is great!

Older Muslim teenagers may be more *au fait* with *Neighbours* or Indian films than with biblical parables, but the same approach applies. A Christian youth leader with a group of Bengali teenagers told me he usually picks a story from a current film as the starting point for a brainstorming session on God. I also remember a discussion with a Muslim family that started with God and ended with *Eastenders*! Shabana asked me how one becomes a Christian and I began laboriously explaining the intellectual concept of being born again. Her father commented: 'That sounds like a Hindu idea'. 'Oh no,' I said, 'it's not reincarnation,' and then dug myself further into a hole with an exposition of Nicodemus in John 3. Finally, it was Shabana herself who cracked it. She interrupted my waffle with: 'Oh, you mean it's like on *Eastenders* . . . Nick's just become a Christian and it's all about saying goodbye to the past, and starting afresh with Jesus in your heart.' I looked at her, stunned! Her lateral thought had communicated exactly what I had wanted to say. We talked late into the night, and I promised to bring an Urdu gospel next time.

Reflect

- *We looked at the story of the woman with a haemorrhage in Ch. 7. Think how you might share other biblical stories about women with your Muslim friends: Moses' mother (Exodus 1, 2), Hannah wants a child (1 Samuel 1, 2), the woman whose daughter was ill (Matthew 15:21–28), Peter's mother-in-law (Mark 1:29), the widow of Nain's son (Luke 7:11–15), Mary Magdalene (Luke 8:2), the lame woman (Luke 13:10–17) and the Samaritan woman (John 4).*

Life's a pageant!

The two-thirds world is not afraid of public events. Life is to be celebrated and shared in the community. Street theatre, puppets, fairs and even the March for Jesus can present Christians with an opportunity to share Jesus in the open air. Several cities have Asian *melas* (fairs) where Christian tracts can be offered in Asian languages.

Discuss

- *How about getting together with other Christians and planning a street event which your Muslim friends would enjoy?*

Reaching the heart of the community

How can the church reach out to whole families in the heart of the Muslim community? Western Christians have grown up with the belief that conversion is an individual decision. Yet a Muslim woman is not her own person. If she is to make a life-changing response to the message of the gospel she will need her husband's approval, otherwise she risks the wrath of family and community. It is difficult for a young British-born woman brought up as a Muslim to become a Christian, but the difficulties are even greater for a middle-aged Muslim woman, born in Pakistan and living a traditional Muslim family life in Britain. There are a few examples around the country of churches where Muslim women who are in their forties, married with children and whose first language is not English have become Christians, been baptised and attend church regularly. Asian Christian fellowships are often very important in the discipleship of such women.

The church has a special ministry to the outcast. Most of those who have come to follow Christ in Britain from a Muslim background have been individuals. Some are already outcasts of their own community, others have become so through conversion. But in view of the strength of the family, is not the ideal for whole families, rather than individuals, to come to faith in Christ together? Perhaps the most effective churches are where there is multicultural leadership and worship, members are from many different cultural backgrounds and the outreach is consistent and long-term.

The challenge then is to the mainstream churches; to ensure we are preaching Christianity not Britishianity, to develop culturally appropriate ways of sharing Christ, to be enriched by Asian expressions of Christianity and 'to become part of the community'. Are we prepared to keep loving our Muslim friends even when they don't convert? Should a Muslim turn up at our church wanting to know Christ, are we prepared for their cultural and personal needs? Is there a need for radical change in the way we do things? Ch. 10 explores these issues further.

Discuss

- *Is our decision to follow Christ an individual one or a family/community one (see Joshua 24:15 and Acts 16:31ff.)? - Are these positions mutually exclusive?*

- *How can we reach out to whole families?*

- *'If you want to witness, you have to become part of the community' (Shuguftah). How much is your church really in touch with the Asian community on the ground? Do your church leaders know the local religious leaders?*

- *What are the everyday issues affecting the Muslim community near your church? - Can you share with them on issues such as racism, abortion, the needs of local schools . . .?*

Notes

1. Revelation 1:5.
2. Vivienne Stacey, *Practical Lessons for Evangelism among Muslims*, p. 22.
3. Compiler of *Ishmael My Brother: A Christian Introduction to Islam*.

4. Though the focus of this book is outreach to Muslims, of course many churches will also have Sikh, Hindu and Buddhist or Jewish neighbours, along with agnostics and atheists. Many training resources are geared towards outreach to other faiths, rather than just Muslims.

5. For further details of this Asian Alpha Course contact Solihull Christian Fellowship or South Asian Concern (see Appendix).

6. Anne Cooper, *Ishmael My Brother*, p. 205.

7. Stacey, p. 9.

8. *Ibid.*, p. 13. Vivienne told the farmers she didn't have carrots in her bag. Everyone's curiosity now aroused, she said she had booklets (these were Christian tracts), which she then passed round. When he read about Jesus, one man said: 'This is foreign seed.' She replied: 'Oh no! It is not foreign seed. It was first sown in Asia.' The conversation continued in this metaphorical way.

9. *Give me your heart* by Adrian Plass, published in Daylight Bible Reading notes (B.R.F.) September–December 1994.

10. See Appendix for Asian language resources.

Women of Courage

Drinking from the well of salvation

This chapter is dedicated entirely to accounts (mainly autobiographical) of Muslim women (and one family) who have searched for and found the truth of Christ. The accounts speak for themselves. Read on to the next chapter for the implications which follow conversion—many implications are for the church!

* * * * *

Closer than a friend

'I'm the only woman I know like me who's done this. You could call me courageous, but actually I've made a lot of wrong choices in my life. We're quite a close-knit Muslim family and our *Ma-ji* is definitely the strong one we all look to. Even through the difficulties of my marriage. And even when my husband left me and the kids, she didn't let me down.

'Life hasn't been easy. I think some would call us a problem family. But, though social services come and go, it's my Christian friends who've always been there for me in the last twenty years. You can't hang around with people and not be attracted by their lives. I suppose I've always been looking for love and affirmation, yes, and forgiveness too, so I looked to my friends to give me this. But eventually I knew it wasn't them I needed but their Jesus.

'In the end it was my overwhelming love for Jesus that overcame my fear of losing *Ma-ji* and I got baptised. It's up to her what the family do to me now. She knows, though, who's stuck by me all these years and who got my family out of a dead-end situation. And she has seen visions of Jesus, so perhaps she'll have the courage to follow him too.'

* * * * *

A hope and a future

'My parents are Muslims who moved in the early 60s from a Pakistani village community to an inner city in northern England, so they could give better educational opportunities to their children. We're working class and we lived in a council house. We were brought up quite strict. To question my dad was really difficult but we did and suffered for it. I had learnt to read the Qur'an in Arabic by the age of eleven (a bit slow!) and fasted and prayed regularly. The whole pattern of my life was set out.

'We were brought up in a home where spirituality was highly valued. This is very different from British material-istic, humanistic upbringing. I wanted to find peace in Islam, so I joined women's groups in the mosque, and read an English translation of the Qur'an. After nine months of this, I decided I couldn't follow all of it. I'm the kind of person to do things a hundred per cent. So I stopped being a Muslim in my heart but my family didn't know.

'When I was eighteen I went to polytechnic. I didn't class myself as a Muslim. I started breaking the Muslim rules; I changed my dress, socialized with both sexes, went to pubs and clubs. Before my nineteenth birthday, a good friend on my course became a Christian. He was born again and didn't we know it! He shared my house so I couldn't escape! He was really lively and zealous, praying all the time. I didn't know much at all about Christianity.

'He asked me a lot of questions about Islam, and we discussed for hours (as students do!). I became defensive, maintaining that Islam was the best thing since sliced bread. As he questioned me, I began to question myself. It never crossed my mind I could be anything else than a Muslim. I had been brought up to believe if you're not a Muslim you're not anything.

'I regard myself as broad-minded, so as an intellectual exercise I decided to get to the bottom of this. I took myself off to the Christian Union. The speaker preached on the peace and love that Jesus can give. I was surprised—"that's not what religion is about", I thought. He gave me an important verse—Jeremiah 29:11ff.: ' "I know the plans I have for you,' declares the Lord, "plans to prosper you and not to harm you, plans to give you hope and a future. Then you will call upon me and come and pray to me, and I will listen to you. You will seek me and find me when you seek me with all your heart. I will be found by you," declares the Lord.' It bowled me over to realize that you can understand the Bible! He gave me his card and asked me to ring him before I became a Christian.

'One day friends invited me to church. J. John[1] was speaking on the subject "Do all religions lead to God?" It was my first time in church. People were singing, clapping and raising their hands—was this church? It felt cultish, bizarre. J. John was saying "I can feel God's presence". I thought "No, no, that can't be!" I agreed that there was only one God, that God is a God of forgiveness, but I got stuck at Jesus dying and being raised and that God could be man. I went home and rang the vicar who had given me his card. I visited him several times and he was very influential in my becoming a Christian. He explained the Trinity, and that God is everywhere, so he could be in church. I was given *I Dared to Call him Father* by Bilquis Sheikh, a noble Pakistani woman who became a Christian (See Appendix). That helped me to see that someone else had done it.

'I went home for Christmas 1987. It was my most depressing holiday at home ever. I was confused. It hit me for the first time that after my degree what followed was marriage, surrounded by my community and extended family. I thought, "I can't do this. There is a greater truth." I knew I couldn't live a hypocritical life as some do. But I felt torn. In Muslim families there is such strong loyalty. My parents had come here for my sake, so I felt obliged to them to live how they wanted me to live. They had given up their country, their culture, everything for the sake of their children. I was terrified.

'In January 1988 I went back to college. I was relieved to be back, and I felt the freedom. Now I could go to church, read the Bible, and talk about Christianity. Yet I struggled. I knew my white Christian friends were praying for me to become a Christian. I battled with their desire for me to come to Christ and my "it's OK for you but you don't understand what it would mean for me". I had to come to God, and say "I have to trust you, that I won't die and you will protect me." I was baptised the following May.

'That was several years ago. I am still a Christian, I am still alive and God has protected me. I needed to rethink my perception of sin and forgiveness, the contradiction of loving God and fearing God. Looking at God as my Father more than some "thing" which is really huge, powerful, Almighty. I also needed healing because I carried a lot of baggage from being a Muslim. Through healing I experienced joy.

'Another joy is always knowing Christ. Knowing that only Jesus has been there, felt it, done it, seen it. I especially felt the power of Christ in my life when I was in my parents' home, with no Bible, no church, no Christian friends, only prayer. It does wonders for your prayer life when you've got nothing else!

'Looking back, I can see God's hand. I can see that he has protected me and has guided my life, as the Psalmist said: "Where can I go from your spirit? Where can I flee from your presence? If I go up to the heavens, you are there; if I make my bed in the depths, you are there. If I rise on the wings of the dawn, if I settle on the far side of the sea, even there your hand will guide me, your right hand will hold me fast."[2]'

★ ★ ★ ★ ★

This challenging account continues at the beginning of chapter ten with a description of the issues and struggles she faced at church.

Facing the minarets

An account by a young woman, brought up as a Muslim in this country, of how she came to know Christ as a young teenager:

★ ★ ★ ★ ★

'I spent the day walking through the streets of my home town. The *azan* (call to prayer) was ringing out of the tannoys from the mosques. The women were hurrying to collect their children from their daily Islamic lessons. I reflected on my own religious upbringing, learning the religion of our forefathers. We were extremely proud of the morality we held and tried to live by, so far removed from the English children we saw. Their obvious freedom of expression confirmed our parents' conception of England.

'I would never have thought then that I would be removed from all this, removed from those I loved and from beliefs that I thought held me secure. But one summer I started having serious doubts. Where was God? Why did he allow all this suffering? God seemed so distant from mankind. At that point of desperation I ploughed into my Qur'anic studies and prayers and yet God was still distant. The *azan* was ringing in my head: *There is no God but Allah and Mohammed is his Prophet.* There was no God for me.

'I started to live my life according to my own rules that weren't dictated by an existence of God. However, that didn't last long. Human endeavours always have their shortcomings.

It wasn't until the December of that year that I realized life did not have to be like this. I was awoken one night by a voice that almost seemed to whisper, speaking into the depth of my heart. There seemed to be a warmth around me. It was so strange. I could not make out where the voice was coming from; there was no one else in my room. The whisper came again. It was such a soft, warm voice, calling my name and saying: "I am the one you've been looking for; I am the way, the truth and the light. No one comes to the Father except through me."

'Those words pierced my heart. They contradicted everything I had been taught. Surely Islam was the only true religion, Allah the only God? "And anyway, Jesus, you're only a Prophet."

'The more I denied it, the more I felt the presence of God. I could feel such immense love around me. That still, small voice called the next night and the night after that. By then I was breaking. There was such sin in my life, yet I was being offered a free gift that would take my burden of sin away and bring me close to God. I knew I had to accept Jesus into my life or I would never get another chance. I whispered: "Jesus, I believe in you. I believe you died for my sins." As soon as I said those words, I felt such release, and a peace I had never known before came over me.

'That was over ten years ago. A lot has happened since then. Relatives have disowned me and zealots have plotted against me. But as I stand facing the minarets I hear a deafening cry of the lost souls of Islam, a cry that will always be heard unless we take up the call to bring them the love of Christ.'

★　★　★　★　★

How I found the 'right' path

An account by a young woman brought up in the UK, with a Pakistani Christian mother and Pakistani Muslim father:

* * * * *

'My mother and father were studying in Pakistan when they met. My father was brought up a Muslim, but made a kind of Christian commitment in the late 50s, early 60s. My mother was from a Pakistani Christian background. They married and came to England where they experienced a lot of difficulties. My parents struggled to get accommodation, and become established in Britain, a foreign land to them. My elder sister was born in 1962 and I was born in 1964. During that time my father went back to Pakistan. It seems that his family persuaded him to return to Islam, telling him that he was leading his daughters to hell.

'He returned to England a different man. He became a devout Muslim and started going to Mecca on an annual pilgrimage. My mother was in a dilemma. She decided as part of her Christian witness to follow her husband's wishes in bringing up the children as Muslims, but she would never change her religion. There followed years of conflict; we girls were made to read the Qur'an every day at a certain time. I hated that because I wanted to be out playing with my friends. I did not understand what I was reading, which frustrated me a lot.

'My parents began to have problems in their marriage. We girls knew whose side we were on, because we observed their different behaviours. My mother submitted to my father, sang and prayed and was even joyful in her difficult situation but my father put his foot down and ordered her around. I grew up with a very negative view of men. I hated Islam, yet at the same time I didn't really know what I was. As a teenager I called myself a "Chruslim" because Mum was a Christian and Dad was a Muslim. In my heart of hearts I knew Christianity was right because Mum was living a good, pure and holy life and Dad wasn't. We girls went to church together but we still came home and carried on swearing, lying, smoking and drinking. All I wanted was to get my A levels, leave home, go to university and be free.

'Then one year we went to a Billy Graham rally and I realized that there was a different kind of freedom; being free to do what was good by becoming a slave of Christ. Probably because of a desire to escape from our problems at home we plunged into church activities. I got such peace and fulfilment from serving God. A year after becoming a Christian, I knew I needed power from God to be able to say to Dad "I'm not a Muslim any more". One evening I was baptised in the Holy Spirit and the next evening the Lord gave me strength to go and tell Dad. That night was a turning point for us. Dad decided he did not want to know us any more. He said "You are dead to me. I have no daughters now."

'Finally, my father divorced my mother and the house was eventually repossessed. As a new Christian I was frightened of the Muslim community. We had been rejected by the Muslim community; friends stopped coming to visit us, they put pressure on us to go back to Islam. People pitied us, saying "Poor old so-and-so, her husband's left her; who's going to marry those daughters now? They'll end up on the streets.

Look at them walking down the street with their legs show-ing." The attitude of Muslim friends and neighbours was that we girls had only become Christians because we wanted to be like white girls, to go out with boys, go to discos, to drink. In actual fact, since I have become a Christian my life has become so much more disciplined; I have become a disciple of Jesus and I know that I can no longer do the things I used to do. If I had remained a Muslim I would still be smoking.

'So we lost our Muslim friends. We lost some of our rights; for example, my father terminated the credit arrange-ment we had with the local shop. I remember my mother telling us that she had been refused credit. I cried and thought "he's even taking the *roti* (bread) from our mouths". Yet God provided jobs for us, and we never wanted for anything. The church became our family and it has been our family ever since. We feel very strongly about friends who have been there from day one. One day, we asked an elder in the church, from a Sikh background, who therefore understands Asian culture, to be our brother, our "*bhai-jan*". We had no brother of our own and our father had left. He was so honoured and readily agreed. Every time there was a prob-lem, or we needed some fellowship or encouragement we would phone him and he and his wife and children would welcome us and offer hospitality.

'During this time we always kept our heads high; we kept our *izzat*. The honour of the family is so important. Asian people think that only having a father or a brother or a male member of the family will keep the honour of the family. But people look on and see that we have kept on the right path. We realized that we were being observed, so it was so much more important that we conducted ourselves properly. We made sure not to go into pubs and discos, so as not to allow people to believe we had become Christians so we could drink and become "white". People now say to both my mother and my father: "You must be proud of your daughters". My father has a respect for us, though he doesn't agree with us.

'One of the things I experienced as a new Christian was that I desperately wanted to find out if there were any other ex-Muslims and I prayed and prayed and prayed: "Lord, there must be other ex-Muslims". I ended up being told about another young woman from another city who had become a Christian from Islam. We became pen friends and wrote to each other about our situations. When eventually we met, that was so enriching; we just hugged each other. This is such an important point: that new converts need to be put in touch with others who have been through the same experience, people of like mind, of the same culture. Being a woman, this friendship was ideal as I could go and stay with her and we would share together, go on walks and go shopping together.

'What I needed most was a spiritual "mum". I had my own mum, but she had her own problems to contend with. I have a friend who is like a second mum to me. She is so knowledgeable in the Word, and taught me so much. She literally discipled me. What is so important in discipleship is consistency; being consistent in meeting up with each other regularly. We prayed together, we went places together, to McDonald's, to town. We hardly ever sat down and had Bible studies. I don't believe that's what discipleship is about; it's actually living your life with that person and helping them by way of example.

'Thinking about other young women who like myself have become Christians, I think we all have certain qualities in common. We are all quite headstrong; we all have that fighting spirit, which I think has helped. We have had the opportunity to be educated and broaden our minds and be involved in employment.

'On the face of it, it may appear that these Muslim converts have made it in life, but people tend to forget how much they have had to leave behind. There may be an aching in their heart because of what they have left behind; because they have been cut off from family members. I ache sometimes because our dad rejected us. I miss him. I wish I had had a Christian dad. I know God's my Father, but at times I would have loved a spiritual father to be there, just to say to me "You're doing the right thing there" or give opinions on things. I envy the positive father-daughter relationships I see in the church.

'So we have come through to follow Christ, but we haven't done it without some sacrifice, some suffering. But the Lord says that if we want to share in his glory, we must also share in his suffering.'

★ ★ ★ ★ ★

The following true story[3] tells of the sequence of events which led a family to flee their native Iran, and finally find faith in Christ.

★ ★ ★ ★ ★

Finding refuge in Christ

Middle-aged Mohammed sat on the plane he had boarded in Istanbul, reflecting on his experiences of the past few weeks since he had left Iran fearing for his life.

He thought about his wife and their five children. He had married Farideh when she was fifteen years old and now their eldest daughter, Mitra, was 25, their only son, Reza, was 23, their daughter Pouran was 21, a third daughter, Zahra, was 8 and the youngest member of the family, Shiva, was 4. They were a highly religious and devoted family; he knew they would not betray him. He hoped they would soon be able to join him.

Mohammed was especially concerned about Zahra's health. She had been a sickly child since birth and the doctors said one of her kidneys wasn't working correctly. They had wanted to remove it, but his wife thought she would not survive the operation. He longed to get her to the West for a reliable second medical opinion.

Mohammed had lived a quiet, ordinary life until the Islamic revolution had changed all their lives for ever. He began to speak out. After all, what threat could a middle-aged Iranian be to an all-powerful dictatorship? But one day he heard they were coming to arrest him. That night he said 'goodbye' to his family and hailed a lift in a truck heading for the border.

Crossing over the mountains into Turkey took several days and nights. Once in Turkey, he was constantly on the watch for the Turkish police. He found someone who sold him a passport on which he could travel to the West, but this used up most of his money and for several days he could buy no food.

Now at last he was on the plane that would take him to freedom, security and a new future. As soon as the pilot announced that they were out of Turkish airspace, Mohammed went to the lavatory, carefully tore up his illegal passport and all his other documents into tiny shreds and flushed them down the toilet.

He settled back into his seat. Suddenly the pilot told them to fasten their seat belts as they were preparing to land. But his joy soon changed to alarm as they realized they were landing not in Sweden, but at Heathrow. He gathered his wits about him and followed the other passengers into the passenger lounge. When an official asked to see his boarding pass, Mohammed had nothing to show him. Though his English was very limited, he understood with difficulty that he would not be going on to Sweden. He decided to apply for political asylum and after lengthy interviews at Heathrow he was allowed to enter the country and given temporary accommodation. The dreams and plans he had had were fast disappearing.

Over the next few weeks he attended English classes but he was no longer a young man and he found it difficult to remember the words. He battled with depression. Would he ever see his family again?

One day he came across a church. Here he heard the same Bible stories his Armenian neighbour back home had told him, and eventually he was put in contact with some Iranian Christians. Life began to get better. He could now meet regularly with fellow countrymen and he increasingly liked what he heard about the gospel and Jesus Christ. One day Mohammed learnt that several of his new friends were being baptised. Still unsure what it was all about he joined them. Soon after his understanding of the Christian faith increased and he accepted the Lord Jesus Christ into his life as his personal Saviour and Lord.

Meanwhile, Mitra had been able to secure a student visa and had joined her father. She had applied for political asylum as soon as she reached England and after a period of a few more months her sister Pouran also managed to join them. After many months a medical visa was secured to bring Zahra, her mother and Shiva to England. The family was overjoyed to be together again and the children were also pleased to hear about their father's new faith.

At first Farideh was very sceptical; she determined to become a better Muslim and resumed her ritual prayers. When she reluctantly agreed to attend the Christian meetings with her family, she was on her guard. But she was impressed by the genuine love and acceptance she felt there. These were her own people. They had suffered in similar ways to herself. They were equally deeply distressed by the chaos that Islam had created in Iran, and, if she was honest, she longed for there to be another way to know God, rather than through the strict Islamic codes of law and practice. Over a period of time she listened to what was being said. Finally she gladly embraced the One about whom she was learning and experienced new life in him.

Pouran and Zahra were keen to learn about the Christian faith and also to learn English, so they began to attend the local lively church. They were made to feel very welcome, and, being open-hearted girls, they readily invited the young people to their home. One of these young people was on the look out for a wife, and, with the arrival of Pouran, felt his search had come to an end. He was a young English lad who had come from a broken home and had never known the security and comfort of a close-knit family. When Pouran's family showed him the welcome and hospitality normally shown to all guests, he took it to mean that they approved of him as a potential son-in-law. Pouran tried to explain this was not the case and gently turned down his marriage proposal. It took time for him to be convinced and much heartache was endured.

But how should Mohammed and Farideh discharge their responsibility towards their daughters and find them suitable partners in a country whose culture is foreign to them and where there is so much potential for misunderstanding?

One such cultural conflict was with the housing department. The department was not happy about the family living together as both Mitra and Pouran were considered to be adults and were therefore entitled to apply for a place on their own. Yet, according to Iranian culture, as single girls they should remain with their parents until they marry. This dilemma caused Mohammed and Farideh much anxiety, and it was eventually resolved by the daughters being housed within walking distance of the family home. Another conflict was with the education authority. The family's application for Zahra to attend a girls-only school was refused, as was their appeal. With great reluctance they sent her to a mixed school, but they are still very worried about this. Why are there not sufficient single sex schools in England to meet the demand for places?

Farideh is now a strong Christian. She has also found hidden character strengths; now she is in the West she is free to develop in a way which would not have been tolerated in Iran. As she grows in her faith she is discovering

her identity and inevitably great tensions result. Mohammed now finds he is married to a strong, independent
woman and his attempts to bring her back into line have
been fiercely resisted. For the first time in her life she can
travel on her own, without a child as chaperone. She can
decide what to do with her time as it no longer takes all
day to prepare meals. She is now insisting on doing the
shopping, something she never did in Iran; the bazaar was
no place for any decent woman to be seen in. Before,
Mohammed never consulted her about finance but now he
is forced to do so.

Farideh is now questioning some of the values she used
to hold dear. She's been married since the age of fifteen and
now she wants some joy and fulfilment out of life. She sees
other western women enjoying easy lives; now it's her turn.
Her existence no longer revolves round her husband and
so it is easy for him to feel superfluous.

Having tasted the freedoms of the West, a return to
traditional Iranian values seems impossible. How impera-
tive it is that before their unique identity is completely lost,
they be helped to acknowledge the many positive facets of
their Iranian heritage and build on them. By coming to
England this family has left behind the threat of imprisonment and death, but they have inherited another set of
problems. How (and how far) do they integrate into the
culture here? Will they always find themselves on the
outside looking in? Will they always feel that their dearly
held cultural values are being undermined? Will they ever
learn the language sufficiently to really understand what is
going on and be able to communicate from their hearts?

Will their children grow up as westerners and eventually deny their heritage? Will they ever be fully accepted by those they live close to and meet at the school gate or in the corner shop? Who are they? Where does their future lie, here or back home in Iran?

Questions, questions. Sometimes they feel they will go mad because of the questions they ask themselves day in, day out. Questions, but very few answers.

★ ★ ★ ★ ★

Notes

1. The Christian evangelist.
2. Psalm 139:7–10.
3. Names have been changed to protect identities.

[10]

Consequences for Converts and the Church

What is it like to be an Asian Christian in a mainly English church? Asian Christians are the ones who can tell us. Two of the women who gave their testimonies in Ch. 9, and two others, were asked what they wanted to say to churches in Britain. Even though each person's account is unique, from different churches and parts of the country, their comments are remarkably similar. Let's see what they have to say.

Shuguftah, whose testimony is on pages 203 to 206, continues her story:

* * * * *

'This is a description of how I feel at times in the Anglican church:

Isolated,
Different.
My mother always told me, however hard I tried
I could never be white, be one of them,
I would always be a coconut;

I could never change the colour of my skin, my identity,
my culture, my roots, me.

Do you know me?
Have you taken the time to know me?
Don't label me as an "Asian Christian".
I am a person who struggles like anyone else;

Yet your convenient caring doesn't know about my struggles
and sacrifices
As I try to serve the Lord in my life.
How it feels when your own mother never phones or writes,
Doesn't know whether you are dead or alive.
When your own community never recognises you
as one of them.
When you're marginalised and isolated because of your faith.

I have left it all;
culture, community and family to be a Christian.
The cost is also to sit alone in church
isolated and marginalised because I am different, an oddity,
someone avoided.

Come and talk to me,
share my struggles, beyond the convenient caring.
Know me.
Then, and only then, you will no longer label me as an
"Asian Christian"
But simply as Shuguftah, your sister in Christ.

'After becoming a Christian I moved to a middle class town in
the south of England. I attended a large Baptist Church but I
felt alienated as I was the only Asian Christian in the church. I
felt pressured into becoming English. It all seemed very English

to go to church in the morning, have Sunday lunch, go for a walk in the afternoon, church in the evening, and house group during the week. I thought: I don't want to be English but I do want to be a Christian. I felt pressurised by Christian friends, who said I wasn't a real Christian because I hadn't told my parents, I hadn't "come out" (though I had told my brothers and sister). It was hard for me to hang on to God.

'I began to question myself, thinking maybe I'm not good enough because I haven't told my parents, I haven't sacrificed everything. I was scared that my parents would find out I had become a Christian, and that my dad would kill me. When I expressed these fears to my friends, they didn't believe me, and accused me of exaggerating. Surely my parents would come round? But no, I wasn't exaggerating. It's hard for people to understand the strong sense of loyalty in the Muslim community. If one person brings shame on the family, it's better to get rid of that person rather than live with them. I felt misunderstood, not accepted by the church. When I wore *shalwar kameez*, people said: "What is that called that you're wearing?" I could say the same to them!

'I didn't stay long in that town. I moved back to the Midlands and stayed with the Anglican church. I have to say it's not because of the church that I'm still a Christian. It's because God's got hold of me. That also causes me sadness. It is a challenge for all of us including me. In the churches there's a great concern for conversion. But will we support them? Get our hands dirty? Be their family? Be their community that they have left? I don't know.

'I began to think God had made a mistake: why aren't my parents Christians like everybody else's? Why hadn't I been to

Pathfinders? I had a deep desire to belong to a family and a community which didn't go away when I became a Christian.

'I have now come to realise that God has made me a mixed cookie for a purpose. Jeremiah says: "I will bring you back to the place from which I carried you into exile".[1] After my degree God carried me back to the country of my parents. I went to Pakistan for a year, with Tear Fund. During that time, God showed me in a deep way that I was an Asian Christian and that here in this community where I lived were lots of Pakistani Christians. For the first time everyone in the church was brown; I wasn't a minority. The church worshipped in Urdu. They sang songs in Punjabi and the Lord's prayer in Urdu. God came into my Asianness. My Asian roots changed in my mind from being a black box, with heaviness and chains that bound me. God freed me to be Asian. He said: "I want you to be Asian. I want you to be able to worship me with your people, in your own language, with people with the same colour skin. I want you to walk into a church in your *shalwar kameez* and for people to say 'that's fine'." One of the joys has been discovering that.'

★ ★ ★ ★ ★

Another young British Asian woman from a Muslim background, agrees:

★ ★ ★ ★ ★

'Family is important. If we say the church is the family of God, we've got to be the family of God. If someone new joins a church and they've just been kicked out of their house, who's going to take that person in? Or who's going to help them and see them through each step of the way, to getting accommodation and other needs? I want to stress: family is important. When a Muslim becomes a Christian they need family replacements. They need a spiritual mum, dad and sisters, and simply a door that's open. A lot of the onus is on the individual to ask for help since church members don't necessarily come forward. They may not recognise the need. Our church has a good foundation, having converts from Islam, Sikhism and Hinduism. I have had a lot of acceptance and love and care, but the understanding wasn't quite there. My support system has been my mother and sister, both of whom are Christians too. We had each other and we clung to that, because we didn't have anyone else.

'My sister said to me one day: "You need to go the pastor's house, knock on the door, go inside his house, sit on the settee and tell him everything. You need to explain to him exactly what you're going through and say: can you pray for me, can you help me, this is what's happening at the moment in my life. I might be there every Sunday morning, hands in the air, but you don't know the pain." If you're in a church where people just pray for you, you don't want to hear that. Yes, prayer is important, but you also need the practical help. You need more than "hello, how are you, see you next Sunday".

'It's hard to get close to people in western culture and even in a close-knit church it is sometimes just the same. If that's the case, the church is taking on board too much western culture; it's going the way of the world. In the New Testament it says that the disciples devoted themselves to prayer, fasting, fellowship, breaking of bread. They broke bread in the homes. My mum, herself an Asian Christian woman, has often visited other

Christian Asian women in their homes to encourage them and pray for them, and now they are holding fellowship meetings in each other's homes. She is also considering opening her home up to adopt an ex-Muslim girl, now that her daughters have left home. Being available and offering ongoing, regular support involves sacrifice but it's so important. People then feel they belong and that they are not abandoned. If you just go to see someone once or say "see you in six months' time", that's no good. If you promise to visit, carry out your promise, don't disappoint them.

'Another important key is to be sensitive to the culture. One example is that you don't have young men going to young women's homes, you don't have a white man going to an Asian woman's home to take her to church. I've experienced that. When my pastor picked us up from home to take us to church, a Muslim neighbour looked at us and spat on the ground. If the pastor's wife had collected us from church, that would have been a lot more sensitive to the culture. Churches can get informed about these issues by reading books, such as the excellent short booklet on Muslim culture, *Salam Alekum* by Frances Iliff or autobiographies of converts.[2]

'It is helpful for churches to hear about a person's conversion first hand. My husband and I went to a church to talk to a group of elderly middle-class white Christians. They were very open and keen to hear our experiences. It helped them to understand that we both originally came from very different backgrounds and cultures (Pakistani Muslim and Indian Hindu). But very few of them had contact with Asian people and they were at a loss as to how to witness to them.

I explained to them that anyone who has become a Christian, from whatever background, is someone who has passed from darkness to light. That is the common denominator we have as Christians, regardless of race, age, sex.

'I explained that Asian people, just like all other human beings, need friends, and if you can befriend your neighbour, or your colleague and just show you care, you can do that for anybody.

'Another major issue is racism and prejudice—from Christians. I was fortunate in that as a young Christian I didn't experience prejudice; it's only since that I have experienced it. I have been misunderstood at times and therefore an opinion has been formed of me which has been wrong, and that's been very hurtful. The person hasn't had the guts to come and talk about it, so I've felt angry that that person has been too frightened to come and approach me. What is so unapproachable about me? Is it the colour of my skin, or is it the way I am, or what? If I had experienced this as a new Christian it might have put me off—I could be a total atheist now. God was good to spare me this early on.'

* * * * *

Bassi Mirzania reminds the church that the last thing a new believer wants is to be put under a spotlight: 'I strongly feel that converts should not be singled out for special treatment. Their pastoral needs will be different from those of the regular congregation and therefore the pastor needs to be aware of their special needs, but they should not be put on a pedestal. Most converts will go through a time of doubt, and consolidation of their faith needs to take place. They need to feel secure enough with someone who can answer their questions and doubts in a reassuring and non-condemning way. I also feel that converts have much to offer to the church and community. They come into the faith with all their life experience, knowledge and talents and they need to be utilised. Their very freshness and new life in Jesus comes like a breath of fresh air through the church and they should be supported as they share their faith.'

Here are some challenging insights from a Pakistani Christian woman in Britain who compares the situation for converts in Pakistan and Britain:

★ ★ ★ ★ ★

Family reaction

'When someone converts from Islam to another religion, it is seen as apostasy, even treachery, since religion and national loyalty are indivisible. If you are born a Muslim you remain so until you die. One mother could not understand when her daughter told her she was no longer a Muslim. "But you are still alive, so of course you are a Muslim!" To deny one's faith heritage is to become, literally, a non-person. There are guidelines in the Qur'an for how to treat an apostate, though there are many different interpretations. One interpretation is that the miscreant should be punished by death.

'In Pakistan, a convert to Christianity from Islam will have more trouble with his family than in Britain. There is a much greater risk that they will take the law into their own hands and get away with it.

'In Britain, although the person may be disowned by their family, they are protected by British law. The family

knows it does not have the power to cause the person to
lose their job. They may threaten loudly to kill the person,
but they are less likely to carry out their threats than in
Islamic countries. It is very likely, however, that they will
turn the person out of the home, and marriage prospects
will be greatly affected. Some converts remain secret believers because their lives would be intolerable otherwise.
This is especially true of young people still under the care
and authority of their parents.'

Isolation

'In Pakistan, a convert will not face immediate loneliness
because in the relational, outdoor, community-oriented
culture of Pakistan, people are not isolated individuals but
share themselves with family, friends and neighbours. Converts can therefore continue to participate in the life of the
community, sitting outside or standing on the street, chat-
ting with passers-by, buying the groceries and being treated
in the usual friendly way.

'In Britain, however, a convert becomes doubly lonely.
They depended so much on their family and community
for security. Once they have been disowned, they suffer
the loneliness of their family's rejection, but as a member
of a minority community they may also find themselves
suddenly alone in the world. It is totally foreign to Asian
culture to be an individual. Every decision is made with
reference to other family members. So in Britain's individualistic culture they will either sink or swim.

'If the person feels very much at ease with western society this may not present an immediate problem. However, many case studies show that even if at first the convert immerses herself in western culture, in the long run she will experience a deep need to rediscover her cultural roots and find out what it means to be a Christian and an Asian. The church needs to be aware of this need, rather than just assuming the convert will be happy to assimilate into western ways.

'All this means it is absolutely necessary for the church to take the convert fully on board and provide a surrogate family and community for her. This is very hard for western Christians to understand, since there is an intellectual divorce between faith and lifestyle. There is no such divide in Asian culture, which is why a convert really is risking losing her life when she turns to Christ.[3]'

* * * * *

This Pakistani Christian goes on to make specific suggestions for the care of converts, many of which concur with the previous accounts.

* * * * *

Family

'If they are made homeless, they will need a surrogate family to provide them with a roof over their head and practical love and care. This is a major and immediate need and cannot be stressed enough. Churches need to rediscover what it means to be the Body of Christ. Members need to be aware that they might need to give in a way they have not been used to giving before. Retired couples whose families have grown up and who are willing to give wise support and care would be ideal.

Hospitality

'Even if not homeless, they will still need the practical love and care of a family or families in the church and be welcomed into family homes (Sunday lunch, cups of tea, an evening just watching TV). One extra person at a meal should not be difficult, and families can take it in turn to provide this for the person. There are so many stories of converts having lost family and friends and then finding that church provides only a once-weekly Sunday morning service and cup of coffee. Even a midweek meeting is not enough. There is a huge need for the person to be grafted into the body of the church and this will involve church members opening up their homes and their lives. The convert needs to be asked how they are, and whether they need money. This may be difficult for westerners who are used to expect the other to assert their own needs. Asians are not used to doing this, and especially so if they are in a critical situation since their needs are so great.

Help according to need

'Most need will be at the beginning. It may be that initially many hours, weeks or months will be needed to help someone, but that they will subsequently need less intensive support.

Married women with children *(See also later section: 'Counting the cost')*

'When a married woman becomes a Christian and is thrown out of the home (with or without her children), the bottom falls out of her world. Such women have an even greater need to be "adopted" by the church. Some may, with a lot of support, manage to live in a council house, but for those who have never led an independent life, this may be a horrifying prospect. Some may have never been to the bank or even got on a bus, and the prospect of making all their own decisions, and closing the door at night to find themselves alone in an empty house can be terrifying. Such women are also very vulnerable to men in the Asian community finding out their situation and plaguing them. There is even a danger that women may end up in bad company or sleeping on the streets.

Shelter

'There is a need for a Christian family centre for women converts and their children. The ethos would be to provide a safe place for a Christian family upbringing and to nurture those young in the faith. It would be flexible according to different needs. Some may need shelter and safety, others may have their own accommodation which is safe but need the love and support of the community during the day or evenings. Children would go to school as normal and come "home" to the centre at night. The members of the community would take it in turns to provide meals and housekeeping and would eat meals together where possible.'

* * * * *

Finally, she raises a point about conversion the other way round:

* * * * *

Why is Islam attracting non-Muslim young people?

'Young western people are being attracted by the hospitality, friendship and love offered by Islam, which they don't see in their family life or in the life of the churches around them. Muslims are seeing their opportunities to offer community to broken families in the white community, especially to teenagers who have never known a secure family life and who are rootless. Young people find that they are given food and tea and told that they can come back again tomorrow. Their Muslim hosts tell them that it is Islam which offers this love and security to them. Actually it is probably truer to say that it is Asian culture, rather than Islam which offers these things. Yet, if western Christians rediscovered their biblical roots they would find that hospitality, loving the stranger and living as a close community in the body of Christ are all fundamental aspects of Christian living and witness. Let's practise it!'[4]

* * * * *

Questions to ponder:

- *What are the major points of need (practical and spiritual) which, according to the above accounts are common to female Muslim converts?*

- *How aware is your church of the needs of a convert?*

- *Would you or your family be able to take in a convert?*

- *Which aspects of Christian culture and church worship might shock someone who was brought up a strict Muslim? - (Refer back to Chs. 4 and 7 in particular).*

- *Could you set up a cell group in your church, aware of these issues and ready to nurture a convert?*

- *What aspects of western cultural church life might enable appropriate help to be given?*

- *'If I had experienced this [racism] as a new Christian it might have put me off'. How can your church be prepared, so as not to put off vulnerable new Christians because of racism in the church?*

- *Should anyone joining an already established church necessarily 'fit in'? Or do you think God might ask the church to change?*

Dilemmas

As already mentioned, the two groups of Muslim females whose conversion brings about particular problems are minor girls and first generation married women. Neither are 'free' agents. In fact, these two categories cover the majority of Muslim women present in Britain today. What options are open to them if they want to follow Christ? Reflect on the following scenarios:

Faith at fifteen

You are the girls' club leader in a successful evangelical church where most members are English. A Muslim girl aged 15 has been coming to the girls' club for some weeks, without telling her parents. One day she professes faith and prays a prayer of commitment. At this stage what would you do and why? Evaluate the following possible courses of action.

1. Advise her to go home and tell her family about her new faith in Christ.
2. Suggest she be baptised in the church in a few weeks' time.
3. Advise she undertake a discipleship training course under your care.
4. Find out which mature female member of the church she feels most comfortable with and link them up for ongoing friendship, support and nurture.
5. Link her with the local Asian Christian fellowship or a local Asian Christian woman.

What are the implications for each course of action?

1. This seems a biblical position[5] but a strong case is made out by some for secret discipleship[6]. There have been cases of children being beaten when they have

professed faith to their parents. If you suggest this to some children of strict Muslim parents this may be the last you see of them. She may be sent to her parents' country of origin for an early marriage.

2. Baptism is an open, public confession of faith. It is questionable whether a few weeks is long enough for either the girl to understand what she has done in accepting Christ, or for you to understand the implications for her future. Since she is a minor, living at home under the authority of her parents, it would be wrong to encourage her to fly in the face of all that her parents have told her about obedience to Islam, the family and community. Would secret baptism be another option at a later stage? Is baptism necessary? [7]

3. Head knowledge alone is not enough. The most important thing is for her and the church to be aware of the full implications of conversion. Unlike the other girls in her group it may mean rejection by her family and Muslim community, possibly physical danger, and greatly reduced marriage prospects. A once-weekly meeting will therefore be nowhere near adequate for her needs. Even if she remains a secret believer for now, she may need to be adopted by a Christian family if and when she does eventually tell her own family. You could consider Vivienne Stacey's *Bible Studies for Enquirers and New Believers* (see Appendix).

4. This may be appropriate to her felt needs. The person may or may not be you! Whoever it is, they need an

understanding of her culture and family situation and great sensitivity. It may well be important to find more than one person, who can offer different kinds of practical support. It is important that the support is on every level, rather than only spiritual.

5. Refer back to the section 'Get multicultural!' in Ch. 8. Whilst still a minor, actual attendance at the meetings may not be possible, but could a friendship with another Asian woman who is a Christian in time help her family see that Christianity is not the 'English' religion? Might a respected older Asian woman be a helpful mediator if and when she eventually tells her family she wants to follow Christ? This building up of trust may take years.

There are other key factors to bear in mind.

Your responsibility towards her and her family

What is the club's policy on parental permission? How do you feel about her coming to the club without her parents' knowledge? How could you get to know the family and build up trust with them? What do you think are the parents' fears about the way the young people in the club behave? How could they be reassured?

Her age and stage

She is still very young. Her attendance at the girls' club may be a sign of spiritual searching; it may also be mixed with her confusion at living two cultural lives (as outlined in Chs. 5 and 8). It is very important for the church to recognise the whole picture rather than just to respond to the spiritual interest which she seems to show at this stage.

Imagine

Imagine you meet the following women. What would be your response to their situations?

- *A Muslim woman from a village in Bangladesh aged twenty-five, married with three children. She has been in the country for three years. She joins mums and toddlers and hears of Christ. She would like her sins to be forgiven and professes faith in Christ.*

- *A Muslim woman, aged thirty-five who has recently left her husband after 19 years of marriage. She has cut her hair short and been seen in the company of non-related men. She has many needs and is very confused. She has not seen her children for several weeks and misses them terribly. In desperation she comes to church and says she wants to become a Christian.*

- *A ten-year-old Muslim girl tells her English friend at school (a member of your girls' club) that her grandmother is very ill and would like the Christians to pray for her. Her grandmother knows that the prophet Jesus is a healer.*

Counting the cost

A Christian woman who has lived in Muslim countries but now lives in England recounts the dilemma her Muslim friend Shaheen faces.

★ ★ ★ ★ ★

'Shaheen lives in a large English city now, but was born in a small village in the subcontinent. She tells me that life was simpler there, things moved more slowly and people had time for each other. She doesn't claim it was idyllic—sometimes there were violent disputes and feuds going on, but she still looks back on it with affection.

'I first met Shaheen when a local Asian organisation put me in touch with her, to help her learn English. We began to meet regularly and a relaxed and easy friendship soon grew between us. As in all friendships, we chatted about all sorts of things, and came to help each other out in different ways.

'One rare occasion when the kids were quiet and the men folk were not around, Shaheen suddenly told me she wanted to talk about Islam. Instead of extolling its virtues, she surprised me by saying how utterly useless Islam was to her; it was something the men talked about but didn't live by. They used it as an excuse to keep their wives subdued; there was much talk about equality and brotherhood, but if you were poor with no connections, there was no equality at all. Women were not welcome at the mosque and she found no respect for her there; she didn't trust the mosque leaders. She doubted whether God really approved of Islam either . . .

'I was stunned by all this, and didn't know what to say.

'Shaheen then went on, pouring out questions: "Tell me about your Christianity; does God answer your prayers? What do you think heaven is like? Your husband doesn't beat you, does he? You go to church with him, don't you?

You are good people, you always help us. We trust you more than our own people."

'Still feeling rather overwhelmed by all this, I tried to answer the questions that kept coming at me. I tried to tell Shaheen that there were well-behaved and badly-behaved people in all religions. I tried to explain that the difference was in what we believed about Jesus, and how we could know God through him. We talked for quite a while, but I wasn't sure how much she really understood me. Then her husband came in and the subject changed. On another occasion her sister Farah joined but her husband, who had heard some of the conversation, came in and gave me a lecture on the superiority of Islam.

'Time passed, and one day I brought some of our family photos to show the sisters. Amongst them were some of an Asian Christian convention we had been to. Shaheen and Farah were fascinated. Were these Asian-looking ladies really Christians? What language did they speak? They had never heard of a church where people dressed and spoke like them and they wanted to see it for themselves. When I suggested that this was possible and I could take them, Farah laughed nervously and said she couldn't. But she encouraged her younger sister to go ahead with it. Shaheen got excited about the idea. Yes, she would go, never mind what her family thought. She would go to a Christian church where she could understand what was being said.

'When I rang the night before we were due to go, it was her teenage daughter who answered the phone. "My mother can't go with you tomorrow." she said. "She's not feeling well." Well, I suppose I had half expected it, and though I was disappointed, I'm ashamed to say that part of me was a little relieved . . .

'When I next visited Shaheen, I asked what had happened. "I wasn't feeling well" she said. But then her true feelings came out: "What would happen if I became a Christian? My family would hate me, my husband would beat me, my children may turn against me or be taken away from me, my community would reject me and call me a traitor. They might not like you any more, either."

'Once again, I was lost for words. I knew the reality of what she was saying. And I had never had to face what she would face in becoming a Christian. What could I say to her? She quizzed me further: "How would English people react if I were Christian? Would they accept me? I'm black, I'll always look different from them. I'd bring them problems, they wouldn't want that. I don't know their language. It's no good thinking about it."

'Very real issues, of course. She was counting the cost— not just considering what she'd lose by rejecting Islam, but wondering what Christianity would bring in its place, socially as well as spiritually. The trouble was that I wasn't very reassuring to her. I should be able to tell Shaheen that if she came to Christ, she would be part of the Body of Christ, with many other brothers and sisters all over the world. That she would have many other Christian friends here in England, not just me, who would enjoy her Asianness, laugh and cry with her, and stick with her even if it brought trouble. That though the cost of following Christ might be high there would be brothers and sisters who would share the cost with her. I would like to tell her these things, but can I?

'Maybe one day, when the kids are quiet and the men folk are out, Shaheen and I will read through some scriptures together and they will speak to her heart. Meanwhile, I am searching my own heart. Why was I secretly relieved when she backed out of coming to the Asian church? Because I fear trouble for her—or for myself? How much am I prepared to share in suffering with Shaheen, should she become a Christian? What form would this take? It would surely be less than hers. Maybe the Asian shops would refuse to serve me? Maybe our family would receive hostility in the street, instead of the warm friendliness we receive now? Would our children be bullied and hounded out of the local park? Would our windows be broken or a mob attack the building? Would secret informers be planted in the church to look out for other "traitors"? Or is my imagination running away with me?

'Shaheen needs to count the cost . . . and so do I. And so does the whole Christian church in the West. I am sure that God is calling the western church to be prepared to "be with" our Muslim friends in all they go through, especially should they decide to follow Christ. It may be costly for us—it will be even more costly for them. But we can remember that there will be joys as well as sorrows. It is God's will for all people to put their trust in Christ. If our Muslim friends come to confess faith in him, it will be God's doing, and it will be a wonderful thing.'

* * * * *

Study

- *Look up the following passages and as you read them, pray for any Muslim women you know like Shaheen, and those you don't know, but who are secretly counting the cost of following Christ. Mark 10:29–30; Isaiah 53:3–4; Matthew 13:45–46; Romans 8:37–39; 1 Peter 4:12–14; 1 Corinthians 12:26–27.*

A radical response: The church as community

Research shows that across the world, 80 per cent of Muslims who convert to Christianity revert to Islam. This is because of the identity crisis they suffer, according to Zafar Ismail, Director of the Open Theological Seminary, Lahore, Pakistan. Having left the security of the Muslim *ummah*, and lost friends, family and community, they suddenly find themselves in a vacuum. Where do they now belong? New converts desperately need to be socialised into their new family and community in Christ otherwise they will be forced to return to their Muslim roots in order to survive.

Since 1982, Zafar Ismail has pioneered the '*biraderi* model' for the resocialisation of converts in Pakistan[8]. A group of Christians in Pakistan looked at the koinonia fellowship model of the early believers at Jerusalem and the house church structures of the Pauline churches. They saw how new believers were cared for and integrated into the community of the church, which became their new *biraderi* (kinship group). By following New Testament patterns for church life, they found that only two or three new converts out of two or three hundred were reverting to Islam. Furthermore, many who previously would have remained secret believers now felt able to make a public declaration.

Christians who have known Muslim converts in Britain have also been forced to re-examine models of church life. What ideas have they come up with? Ralph Neighbour's *Where Do we Go from Here? A Guide Book for the Cell Group Church* (See Bibliography) outlines a similar idea to the *biraderi* model, whereby the cell group is made the basic unit of the church. Cell group members have a commitment to each other to 'be church' to each other throughout the week, coming together with other cell groups on a Sunday for corporate worship.

The house church movement with its New Testament model of a strong support structure and close fellowship provides for many of a convert's needs, but though this model is biblically-based, the culture in which it is clothed may not be appropriate to those from a strict Muslim background.

Does there need to be a more radical rethinking of the church's structure, for the sake of those outside it? A church which has turned its structure upside-down to be relevant to the culture of the non-churched is Willow Creek in USA. Here the main Sunday meeting is geared towards the non-believer and the body of believers has its meeting during the week.

Others want to revive western theology. Has the western evangelical movement lost sight of its heritage? Can the theology of Celtic Christianity, with its emphasis on community, incarnational mission and the supernatural world provide a bridge across which the good news can travel to folk Islam?

Discuss

- *What changes would the adoption of the above models bring about in your own church?*

- *Study the New Testament structures in the book of Acts: how far is it possible to model our church life in modern Britain on these structures?*

- *It has been said that God gives a church only the number of new believers it is ready to support. Do you agree? Is this why our churches have seen so little fruit from evangelism? Let's pray for God to change us and mould us into his 'multicultural body' here on earth.*

Notes

1. Jeremiah 29:14.
2. See Appendix.
3. See Luke 18:28–29 and Mark 8:35.
4. Another urgent issue for Christians is how to support western women who are attracted to Islam and marry Muslim men. Such women may be attracted to the clear roles for women in Muslim family life. Some convert; others do not. If they are a second wife under Muslim law their legal rights may be slim. Either of the wives may be the legal wife according to British law. Whilst some of these mixed marriages may work, there is evidence that a very high proportion break down. Some may involve domestic violence. Disputes may occur over the religious upbringing of the children, family planning or the role of the in-laws. Are Christian women who have some knowledge of Muslim family life able to offer support to such women?

5. See Romans 10:9 and Matthew 10:32–33.
6. Reflect on Nicodemus in John 3 who came at night, Joseph of Arimathea in John 19:38–39 and Naaman in 2 Kings 5:17–19.
7. As seems so in Mark 16:16.
8. Zafar Ismail's article 'What About the Muslim Convert?' was published by Lausanne Committee for World Evangelization in *World Evangelization* No. 69, (December 94/January 95). It is also available on the Internet at http://www.goshen.net/lausanne.

[11]

The Suffering God
Ida Glaser

'If it weren't for Jesus, God wouldn't be like that.'

Haneefa's husband cheated on her. He went to Pakistan and married a girl younger than his eldest daughter, without even telling her. Now, he will divide his time between Pakistan and Britain, and his social security money between two families. There's nothing at all that Haneefa can do about it.

Zainab went to Bangladesh to get married to her cousin. It was an arranged marriage, but Zainab was happy to abide by her parents' choice, and rapidly fell in love with her bridegroom. After three weeks, she returned to England to apply for a visa for him to join her. Two years and more than a thousand pounds of legal fees later, she is still waiting for him, her room full of his photographs. Her cousin had to wait five years before her husband could join her.

Fatima has completed her GCSEs, but with little success. She would like to go on to the sixth form or to a local college, but her parents will not permit it. They do not want her to marry just yet, so she is stuck at home, cooking and cleaning and gossiping with the neighbours. 'Life's boring,' she says. 'Cooking and cleaning are OK, but I'd like to get out and do other things.'

Nasreen's mother-in-law has come to visit. She doesn't approve of the way that Nasreen cares for her husband and children. Everything is wrong. Now, Nasreen's husband is taking his mother's side and criticising his wife. He is even threatening to divorce her.

These are some of my Muslim friends. I know of many other women who are not Muslims but share similar plights and I know many other Muslim women who have no such problems. Yet these friends make me feel helpless, and it seems appropriate towards the end of this book to reflect: 'What does God think of all this? Does he care?' I turn to Scripture, and I find that he does care: he sees, he comes, he suffers and he saves, because that is what he is like.

I recall a conversation with another Muslim friend, a girl of only fifteen. We were talking about the difficult things in our lives, and our times of real suffering. We shared where we felt that God fitted in, and it was clear that my experience was very different from hers. Eventually, I told her about Jesus' entering and transforming our sufferings through the cross, and she made one of the most profound observations I have ever heard: 'You mean, if it weren't for Jesus, God wouldn't be like that?'

And that is the key: if Jesus could be removed from the Trinity, God would not be the One who comes, who suffers and who saves. He might see, but it would be a different seeing, because it would be a seeing without sharing. It is the God who sees, who comes, who suffers and who saves that my Muslim friends need; and that is the God and Father of our Lord Jesus Christ.

Seeing

Again and again through the gospels, Jesus sees the plight of women.

- He sees Mary's longing for spiritual learning (Luke 10:38–42). While her sister expects her to take the conventional female domestic role, Jesus admits her to the conventionally male circle of disciples.
- He sees the injustice offered to the woman taken in adultery (John 8:1–11). While the male accusers—perhaps including her partner in the adultery—thirst for her blood, Jesus convicts them of their own sin, and offers her forgiveness and new life.
- He sees right into the life of the lonely Samaritan woman (John 4:1–26), yet engages her in serious conversation. He brings her secrets into the open, and reveals himself to her as the promised Messiah.
- He sees the destitution of the widow who has lost her only son (Luke 7:11–15), and restores him to her without even being asked.

God has always been like that

Again and again in the Old Testament, God is the one who cares for the vulnerable—for the widow, the fatherless and the stranger. One of the most striking examples is Hagar, the mother of Ishmael, from whom the Arabs trace their descent.

Hagar was a stranger—an Egyptian. She had no husband and, it seems, no family near her. She was a servant, a member of Abraham's household and totally dependent on him and on her mistress, Sarah. She was caught up in the need for a male heir for Abraham, and Sarah's longing for a son—a familiar situation in many Islamic cultures. Sarah urged her husband to follow the local custom of producing an heir through her servant, and, when Hagar gave birth to a son, jealousy ensued. Again, we are not far from the idea that a Muslim man can take a second wife in order to have sons.

Hagar is then thrown out. Sarah shows us that it is not only men who can oppress and exploit women. She, more than Abraham, treats Hagar as something she owns, and seems not to see her humanity.

But God sees. He does not remove her problems, but sends her back to Sarah. Yet she worships him because he sees her—not as goods to be exploited, but as a precious human being. She calls him, 'The God who sees me', and the well beside which she met him, 'the well of the living one who sees me' (Genesis 16:13–14).

That is the first message that we have for our Muslim women friends: God sees. He knows all about you. He sees your needs, your longings, your sins, and the injustices that you suffer. And he sees YOU—not just as the wife of your husband, the daughter of your father, the mother of your sons, but as a precious human being in your own right.

Coming

Most Muslim women will agree so far. They know that God sees them, and they know that his names include *Al-Basir*: 'The See-er', *Al-Sami*: 'The Hearer', *Al-'Alim*: 'The Knower'. The Qur'an (Sura 50:16) tells us that God is closer to us than our jugular vein.

But the knowing and the seeing are different. The God of the Bible does not see from afar, nor is his seeing an attribute due to his power. His closeness is not only one of knowledge, but of coming to be with us. Hagar knew that God had seen her because the angel of the Lord came to her. Genesis records that he 'found her near a spring in the desert' (16:7). This appears to be the first theophany (showing of God) in the Bible, for Hagar recognises that she has actually met with God: 'I have seen the One who sees me,' she says (16:13). God was in the angel, seeking for the lost, outcast woman, coming to her and speaking with her.

God has always been like that

As far back as Genesis 3, the beautiful picture of God walking in the garden (3:8) shows him coming to seek the shameful, fearful, hiding Adam and Eve, finding them and speaking with them. His voice echoes down the centuries before Christ:

> I will be with you (Exodus 3:12).

> I will put my dwelling place among you (Leviticus 26:11).

> The Lord your God will be with you everywhere you go (Joshua 1:9).

> My dwelling place will be with them (Ezekiel 36:27).

> Suddenly the Lord you are seeking will come to his temple (Malachi 3:1).

God is like that in Christ

Muslims will tell us that God cannot come to earth, for he is too great, and too far above us. He is not like us at all. Yet the message we have for Muslim women is that God is even greater than they think. He can transcend even his own transcendence, to come and be with us, and he has done that in the Lord Jesus. As the angel came to the outcast Hagar at the spring, Jesus came to the outcast Samaritan woman at the well. As God came to sinful Adam and Eve in the garden, he came in Christ to a world of sinful, shameful, fearful human beings: he came to us.

It is because he is with us that he sees us. He sees us as human beings because he has come as a human being. He knows what life is like.

This is the next thing we want to share with our Muslim friends: God is with us, here and now. And we, who follow the God who comes, are also with them. We may not be able to help them in any obvious way, but we can draw alongside them as fellow human beings. We can share the comfort that God has given us.

Suffering

The God who comes knows what life is like: he also knows what death is like. We read in Hebrews that:

> In bringing many sons to glory, it was fitting that God, for whom and through whom everything exists, should make the author of their salvation perfect through suffering (2:10).

> During the days of Jesus' life on earth, he offered up prayers and petitions with loud cries and tears to the one who could save him from death, and he was heard because of his reverent submission. Although he was a son, he learned obedience from what he suffered and, once made perfect, he became the source of eternal salvation for all who obey him (5:7–9).

> He had to be made like his brothers in every way, in order that he might become a merciful and faithful high priest in service to God, and that he might make atonement for the sins of the people. Because he himself suffered when he was tempted, he is able to help those who are being tempted (2:17–18).

Jesus, who the New Testament says is 'God with us' (Matthew 1:22), had to suffer and learn obedience in order to be perfect. This does not mean to say that he was disobedient or had any fault—the biblical witness is that he was without sin. It means that, in order to complete his work, he had to be put into situations where he had the possibility of disobedience, and of avoiding the suffering to which he was called. The word 'perfect' here implies just that: completeness, fullness or maturity.

Without this suffering, he could not complete his work. His suffering and his temptations to disobedience mean that he understands our human weaknesses and agonies because he has experienced them himself. He needed to experience them in his life on earth, because sharing our sufferings is part of the character of God.

God has always been like that

As far back as Genesis 6, we read of God responding to the mess in his world with grief and pain:

> The Lord saw how great man's wickedness on the earth had become, and that every inclination of the thoughts of his heart was only evil all the time. The Lord was grieved . . . and his heart was filled with pain (6:5–6).

This is the first glimpse into the very heart of God in the Bible.

The word used for God's pain has the same root as those used of human suffering and pain following the fall in Genesis 3:16–17, and 5:29. It is a word used 'to express the most intense form of human emotion, a mixture of rage and bitter anguish.'[1]

What is it that causes this grief and pain? The immediate context is that:

the sons of God saw that the daughters of men were beautiful, and they married any of them they chose . . . The Nephilim were on the earth in those days—and also afterwards—when the sons of God went to the daughters of men and had children by them (Genesis 6:2,4).

Understanding of these verses is often hidden behind discussions of who the 'sons of God' and the 'Nephilim' were; but there are some things that are clear. The 'sons of God (*elohim*)' might have been heavenly beings, or, more likely, sons of rulers: they were certainly powerful males. The 'daughters of men (*adam*)' were certainly human females, and the powerful men saw that they were beautiful. The word for 'beautiful' is 'good', as used when God looked at his creation in Genesis Ch. 1 and saw that it was 'good'.

So, these powerful men recognised the 'goodness' of the women that God had made; but, unlike Adam who welcomed his wife as 'bone of his bone', they 'married any of them that they chose'. The implication is that they grabbed them and exploited them for their own purposes. The results of these unions were the Nephilim. Whoever they were, they were abnormal—giants, perhaps. They were distortions of God's good creation.

It is this misuse and distortion of his creation that first provokes God's grief and pain, and leads to the corruption and violence of Genesis 6:11.

Orthodox Islam tells us that God does not suffer—he is independent, and human beings cannot harm him in any way. A frequent Qur'anic phrase that describes the result of our sin is 'We have wronged ourselves' (e.g. 7:23): it is ourselves and other human beings that we hurt, and not God.

The Bible records God's personal anguish over his creation when it goes wrong:

> Is not Ephraim my dear son, the child in whom I delight? Though I often speak against him, I still remember him. Therefore my heart yearns for him; I have great compassion for him, declares the Lord (Jeremiah 31:20).

> How can I give you up, Ephraim? How can I hand you over, Israel? . . My heart is changed within me; all my compassion is aroused (Hosea 11:8).

God's pain grows out of his great love for us. This is seen supremely in the Lord Jesus Christ on the cross. It is here that God with us suffers. It is for this that he came. It is from the cross that he sees the need of those around him.

- He sees the weeping women who grieve for him. As he faces his own death, he sees their coming misery, and gives it priority over his own (Luke 23:26–31).
- He sees his widowed mother, about to lose her oldest son. From the midst of his pain, he provides a son for her in the young disciple who is about to lose his beloved master (John 19:25–7).
- He sees the criminals beside him, and assures one of forgiveness and paradise (Luke 23:42–3).
- He sees perplexed, weeping Mary, and comes to give her the good news of his resurrection (John 20:10–17).

This, too, we want to share with our Muslim friends. The God who sees us and has come to us knows not only our weakness but also our deepest hurts. He understands completely. He has not left us alone in our suffering, but has joined us. He is not unscathed by this world gone wrong: he finds it even more painful than we do. He does not seek to escape, but chooses to suffer.

Saving

Jesus did not suffer only to be with us, and so that he could understand and share our sufferings. That would not have helped us. Of what use is it simply to know that someone else suffers as much as we do? If that person is God incarnate, it would merely make life worse. It would mean that even the Most High, the Almighty, was weak and helpless like us. It might lead us into despair.

But the Lord incarnate did not suffer like that. He died not because he was defeated by death, but because he was defeating it. He was not helpless in the face of his sinful creatures: he chose to put himself at their mercy, in order that he might have mercy on them.

This is the Good News. This is the heart of what we have to share with our Muslim friends. This God, the One who sees, the One who comes, the One who suffers, is also the One who through his coming and his suffering has opened the way to salvation for us. By his wounds, we are healed.

Islam teaches that this is unnecessary. Human beings, it tells us, are not sinful but wayward and ignorant. We have not 'fallen': nothing has gone fundamentally wrong with us, and God can simply choose to forgive us and admit us to Paradise if he so wishes. The Bible's diagnosis is much more radical. It sees us as 'dead' and cut off from God because of our sin. That is why he has to come to us—we cannot get to him ourselves. That is why he has to suffer—our sin is so serious that it costs him something to put it right. That is why he has to save—we need him to turn us around and remake us.

There is one positive thing about the plight of many Muslim women who are struggling with the tensions between their families' cultures and the 'West': their problems make it obvious that the world has gone wrong. As we seek to introduce them to this God who sees, who comes and who suffers, let us pray that he will show them where they need saving and remaking. For here is the hope for them, and for their families. Here too is the hope for us and for the whole of our British society and for all of God's creation.

'Jesus is the image of the invisible God, the firstborn over all creation . . . For God was pleased to have all his fullness dwell in him, and through him to reconcile to himself all things, whether things on earth or things in heaven, by making peace through his blood, shed on the cross' (Colossians 1:15, 19–20).

Notes

1.   G.J. Wenham, *Genesis 1–15,* p. 44.

Postscript

So, you've read the book! What do you do now?

From here you can:

- Read some (if not all!) of the books in the Bibliography and further reading list.
- If you haven't done so already, join or form a prayer group to pray for Muslim neighbours.
- Study one of the courses listed in the Appendix.
- Obtain Asian language resources (see Appendix).
- Join an organisation involved in outreach and social justice (see Appendix).
- Join a professional group such as the Association of Christian Teachers or Christians in Education or form a local group.
- Join a Home Tutor Scheme for teaching English (see Appendix).
- Enjoy making friends!

Bibliography

Commission for Racial Equality, *The Sorrow in my Heart: Sixteen Asian Women Speak about Depression* (CRE: London, 1993).

Cooper, Anne (compiler), *Ishmael My Brother: A Christian Introduction to Islam* (MARC: Tunbridge Wells, revised edition, 1993).

Elmer, Duane, *Cross-Cultural Conflict: Building Relationships for Effective Ministry* (IVP: Illinois, 1993).

Evangelical Alliance, *A Celebration of Faith: A Christian response to celebrating religious festivals in schools* (London, 1993).

Haneef, Suzanne, *What Everybody should Know about Islam and Muslims* (Kazi Publications: Lahore, 1979).

Hitching, Bob, *McDonalds, Minarets and Modernity: The Anatomy of the Emerging Secular Muslim World* (Spear: Sevenoaks, 1996).

Home Office Research and Statistics Directorate, 'Ethnic Minorities, Victimisation and Racial Harassment', *Research Findings* 39 (August 1996).

Home Office, *Taking Steps: Multi-agency responses to racial attacks and harassment* (The 3rd Report of the Inter Departmental Racial Attacks Group, 1996).

Ismail, Zafar, 'What About the Muslim Convert?' *World Evangelization* 69 (December 94/January 95).

Khan, Amil, 'Angst on the way to the altar', *Q News* (16–22 August 1996).

Lewis, P, 'Cross-cultural counselling: how far should you enter the world of assumptions of those for whom demon possession (jinn/bhut) is still part of the explanatory system?' (Unpublished paper, 1989).

Menefee, Samuel Pyeatt, *Wives for Sale: An Ethnographic Study of British Popular Divorce* (Blackwell: Oxford, 1981).

Molteno, Marion, *A Language in Common* (The Women's Press: London, 1987).

Musk, Bill, *Touching the Soul of Islam: Sharing the Gospel in Muslim Cultures* (MARC: Crowborough, 1995).

Neighbour, Ralph, *Where Do we Go from Here? A Guide Book for the Cell Group Church* (Touch Publications, Houston, 1990).

Office for National Statistics, *Social Focus on Ethnic Minorities* (ONS: London, 1996).

Parshall, Phil, *New Paths in Muslim Evangelism* (Baker Book House: Michigan, 3rd printing, 1984).

Raleigh, Dr Veena Soni, 'Suicide Patterns and Trends in People of Indian Subcontinent and Caribbean Origin in England and Wales', *Ethnicity and Health* 1:1, (1996).

Shaw, Alison, *A Pakistani Community in Britain* (Blackwell: Oxford, 1988).

Stacey, Vivienne, *Practical Lessons for Evangelism among Muslims* (Interserve: London, rev. English edn., 1988).

Thanvi, Maulana Ashraf Ali, *Bahishti Zewar (Heavenly Ornaments)*, tr. Maulana Farid-Uddin (Taj Company: Delhi, rev. edn., 1992).

Wallis, Jim, *The Soul of Politics* (Fount: London, 1995).

Wenham, G.J., *Genesis 1–15* (Word Books: Texas, 1987).

Appendix

Further Reading

Stories of Muslim Converts

Masood, Steven, *Into the Light* (OM/Interserve: Bromley, 1986). A personal testimony by a Pakistani Muslim who found Christ.

Sheikh, Bilquis, *I Dared to Call him Father* (Kingsway: Eastbourne, 1978). The autobiographical account of the conversion of a noble Pakistani Muslim woman, giving a fascinating insight into Pakistani society.

Wilson, Christy, 'Costly Discipleship: Two Stories from Iran', *Evangelical Review of Theology*, 20:2 (April 96).

Christian Outreach to Muslims

Burness, Margaret, *What do I say to my Muslim friends?* (Church Missionary Society: London, 1989). Role plays for group work, especially for Christian women with Muslim friends.

Chapman, Colin, *Cross and Crescent: Responding to the Challenge of Islam* (IVP: Leicester, 1995). Can be used alone, or as leader's handbook for the course by the same name (see 'Courses' below).

Cooper, Anne, *Heart to Heart: Talking with Muslim Friends* (Word of Life: Oldham, 1997). Available from Word of Life, PO Box 14, Oldham OL1 3WW.

Fitzsimons, Lionel, *Not at Home* (Good News Broadcasting Association/L. Fitzsimons: Doncaster, 1991, reprinted 1996). Available from SIM, Ullswater Crescent, Coulsden, Surrey CR5 2HR.

Gidoomal, Ram, *Sari 'n' Chips: Asian + Western Culture?* (Monarch: Crowborough, 1993). Available from South Asian Concern. See 'Relevant Christian Organisations' below.

Gidoomal, Ram and Fearon, Mike, *Karma 'n' Chips: The New Age of Asian Spirituality* (WPC: London, 1994). Available from South Asian Concern. A sequel to *Sari 'n' Chips*.

Goldsmith, M. and Harley, R, *Who is my Neighbour? World Faiths and Christian Witness* (Scripture Union: London, 1994).

Hayward, Lorna G, *A Practical Guide to Asian Languages in Britain* (FEEL Publications: Birmingham, 1st edn. 1993). Available from 86 Henshaw Road, Small Heath, Birmingham B10 0SX. This book covers a broad range of languages spoken in Britain, from Chinese to Romany.

Hooker, Roger and Lamb, Christopher, *Love the Stranger* (SPCK: London, 1986). Particularly helpful on reaching out sensitively to Sikhs and Hindus.

Iliff, Frances, *Salam Alekum! Understanding Muslim Culture* (Interserve: London, 1995). A practical booklet covering many areas of life and custom.

Mallouhi, Christine, *Mini-Skirts Mothers & Muslims: Modelling Spiritual Values in Muslim Culture* (Spear: Tunbridge Wells, 1993).

Musk, Bill A., *The Unseen Face of Islam: Sharing the Gospel with Ordinary Muslims* (MARC/EMA: Eastbourne, 1989). A very useful study of the practices of folk Islam.

Musk, Bill A., *Passionate Believing: The 'Fundamentalist' Face of Islam* (MARC: Crowborough, 1992).

Stacey, Vivienne, *Bible Studies for Enquirers and New Believers* (V. Stacey: Paphos, 1994). Available from Interserve.

Women in Islam

Afkhami, Mahnaz (ed.) *Faith, Freedom, Women's Human Rights in the Muslim World* (IB Tauris: London, 1995).

Ahmad, Khurshid, *Family Life in Islam* (The Islamic Foundation: Leicester, 6th printing, 1993).

Ahmed, Leila, *Women and Gender in Islam* (Yale University Press: New Haven, Conn., 1992).

Bashier, Zakaria, *Muslim Women in the Midst of Change* (The Islamic Foundation: Leicester, Seminar Papers 5, 4th printing, 1990).

Beck, Loui and Keddie, Nikki (eds.), *Women in the Muslim World* (Harvard University Press: Cambridge, Mass., 1978).

Engineer, Asghar Ali, *The Rights of Women in Islam* (C. Hurst & Company: London, 1992).

Fernea, Eliz. W. (ed.), *Women and the Family in the Middle East* (University of Texas: Austin, 1985).

Glaser, Ida and John, Napoleon, *Partners or Prisoners?* (Paternoster: Carlisle, 1997). A groundbreaking analysis and comparison of gender issues in Islam and Christianity.

Goodwin, Jan, *Price of Honour* (Little, Brown & Co Ltd: London, 1994).

Khayyat, Al Sana, *Honour and Shame* (Saqi Books: London, 1990).

Lemu, B. Aisha and Heeren, Fatima, *Women in Islam* (The Islamic Foundation: Leicester, 2nd printing, 1992).

Mernissi, Fatima, *Women and Islam* (Blackwell: Oxford, 1991).

Parshall, Phil, *Inside the Community: Understanding Muslims through their Traditions* (Baker Books: Grand Rapids, 1994). See chapter on Women.

Stacey, Vivienne, *Women in Islam* (Interserve: London, 1995). The fruit of forty years in Asia and the Middle East.

Stowasser, Barbara F, *Women in the Qur'an: Traditions and Interpretations* (OUP: New York, 1994).

Sociological Studies

Ballard, Roger, *Desh Pardesh (At Home Abroad)* (C. Hurst & Co: London, 1994). A study of Asian settlement in Britain.

Bausch, William J, *STORYTELLING: Imagination and Faith* (Twenty-Third Publications: Mystic, Connecticut, 8th printing, 1993). A book of and about stories (not specific to Muslim women).

Early, Evelyn, *Baladi Women of Cairo* (Lynne Rienner Publishers: Boulder & London, 1993). A book about Muslim women and storytelling.

Jeffery, Patricia, *Frogs in a Well: Indian Women in Purdah* (Zed Press: London and New Jersey, 1979).

Lewis, Philip, *Islamic Britain* (I B Tauris: London, 1994). A study of the issues facing the various religious groupings and the different generations of Muslims in Britain today.

Mirza, Kauser, 'The Silent Cry: Second Generation Bradford Muslim Women Speak', *Muslims in Europe Research Papers* 43, (CSIC, Selly Oak Colleges: Birmingham, 1989).

Murphy, Dervla, *Tales from Two Cities: Travels of Another Sort* (Penguin: London, 1989). A fascinating account of Dervla Murphy's insight into inner-city Bradford and Birmingham.

Sharif, R, 'Interviews with Young Muslim Women of Pakistani Origin', *Muslims in Europe Researach Papers* 27 (CSIC, Selly Oak Colleges: Birmingham, 1985).

Watson, Helen, *Women in the City of the Dead* (C. Hurst & Co: London, 1992). A book about Muslim women and storytelling.

Watson James L. (ed.), *Between Two Cultures: Migrants and Minorities in Britain* (Blackwell: Oxford, 1977).

Wilson, Amrit, *Finding a Voice: Asian Women in Britain* (Virago: London, rev. edn. 1984).

Racial Justice

A Time To Act, (Racial Justice and the Black and Third World Theological Working Group, London, 1992). Available from Evangelical Christians for Racial Justice. See 'Relevant Christian Organisations'.

Haslam, David, *Race for the Millennium* (Church House Publishing: London, 1996). Available from the Churches' Commission for Racial Justice. See 'Relevant Christian Organisations'.

Wright, Fred, *The Cross Became a Sword* (RW Publishing: Harpenden, 1995). Available from Reconciliation Walks, PO Box 61, Harpenden AL5 4JJ.

Hinduism and Sikhism

Wardell, Margaret and Gidoomal, Ram, *Chapatis for Tea: Reaching your Hindu Neighbour: A Practical Guide* (Highland: Guildford, 1994).

Wardell, Margaret and Gidoomal, Ram, *Lions, Princesses and Gurus: Reaching your Sikh Neighbour* (Highland: Guildford, November 1996).

Courses

Cross and Crescent: Responding to the Challenge of Islam by Colin Chapman (CMS, 1996). A 5-session course with corresponding workbook based on the book of the same title. Order the workbook direct from CMS, Partnership House, 157 Waterloo Road, London SE1 8UU.

Culture to Culture. Includes 'Entering Another's World' module: St John's Extension Studies, Bramcote, Nottingham NG9 3DS Tel: 0115-925-1117.

Language Acquisition Made Practical. Language teaching method by E.Thomas and Elizabeth Brewster (Lingua House, 1976).

Multi-faith Britain. House group course (CPAS Church Leadership Pack) by Ida Glaser. Available from CPAS, Athena Drive, Tachbrook Park, Warwick, CV34 6NG Tel: 01926-334242.

Through Asian Eyes. An exciting new open learning course in ministry and mission from an Asian perspective. Details from South Asian Concern, PO Box 43, Sutton, Surrey SM2 5WL Tel: 0181-661-9198, which has produced the course in partnership with Spurgeon's College.

Training Course in Islamics (All Nations Christian College, Easneye, Ware, Herts SG12 8LX). The college runs an annual ten-day introductory course in December.

Word of Life Bible Correspondence Course (Word of Life, PO Box 14, Oldham OL1 3WW Tel/fax: 0161-628-4051). For Muslim enquirers, also for Christians to understand the sorts of questions Muslims ask.

Videos

Coming to Britain: An Immigrant's Story (Christian Television Association, 1996). This video version of Ram Gidoomal's *Sari 'n' Chips* is available from South Asian Concern.

Good Neighbours, (Crosslinks, 1987) Available to hire or buy from Crosslinks. See 'Relevant Christian Organisations'.

Mixed Blessings, (CVG, 1994). An upbeat look at issues for Asians living in Britain. CVG TV, First House, 1 Sutton Street, Birmingham B1 1PE Tel: 0121-622-1337.

Out of the Shadows: An Audio-visual History of the Black Presence in Britain 1500–1950 (Catholic Association for Racial

Justice:1988) St Vincent's Community Centre, Talma Road, Brixton, London SW2 1AS Tel: 0171-274-0024.

Through Their Eyes, (Interserve, 1989). An excellent introduction to the South Asian presence in Britain. The compelling first section 'Just the Same' tackles racial prejudice.

Women in Islam, (Islamic Media Services, Rayan Productions, 1991). Muslim women share their experiences of Islamic life and faith.

Audio Recordings

Language Recordings (UK). Provides basic evangelism and Christian teaching materials in many languages, including a number of majority and minority languages that Muslims may speak (e.g. Sylheti). Write for more information to PO Box 197, High Wycombe, Bucks HP14 3YY Tel: 01494-485414.

Songs of the Kingdom and *Asia Worships*. Asian Christian worship tapes/CDs from South Asian Concern. Both albums have a combination of Eastern and Western styles and tempo.

World Cassette Outreach. 8 Pine Close, Killamarsh, Sheffield S31 8GJ Tel: 0114-248-9563. New Testaments, gospels and the Life of Christ on cassettes, available in several languages.

Resource Centres

Asian Books c/o South Asian Concern. Holds several hundred different resource materials for Asian outreach.

Faith to Faith Resource Centre, 10 Church Lane, Oldham, Greater Manchester OL1 3AN Tel/fax 0161-628-4051. Books, audio tapes in Asian languages and videos for sale or hire.

St Andrew's Book Shop, St Andrew's Road, Plaistow, London E13 8QD Tel: 0171-474-0743. Fax: 0171-511-4874. Book shop and mail-order catalogue service.

The Well, Asian Information and Advice Centre, 48/50 Albert Road, Glasgow, G42 8DN Tel/fax 0141-424-4523. E-mail: info@the-well.demon.co.uk.

For information on resources and local training courses in the West London area contact Stephen Moody, 10 Grosvenor Road, Hounslow TW3 3ER Tel: 0181-572-2171.

Relevant Christian Organisations

Alliance of Asian Christians: Carrs Lane Church Centre, Carrs Lane, Birmingham B4 7SX Tel: 0121-633-4533. Exists to build bridges between all ethnic minority congregations and with the historic churches.

Churches' Commission for Racial Justice: Council of Churches for Britain and Ireland, Inter-Church House, 35–41 Lower Marsh, London SE1 7RL Tel: 0171-620-4444. The CCRJ is involved in topical campaigning including refugee rights, and produces publications on issues such as racial harassment. Their journal is *Church and Race*, produced three times a year.

Crosslinks: 251 Lewisham Way, London SE4 1XF Tel: 0181-691-6111.

Evangelical Christians for Racial Justice: 111 Homerton High Street, London E9 6DL.

ISCS (International Student Christian Services): 3 Crescent Stables, 139 Upper Richmond Road, London SW15 2TN Tel: 0181-780-3511.

MAB (Ministry among Asians in Britain): A Ministry of Interserve c/o 325 Kennington Road, London SE11 4QH. Tel: 0171-735-8227.

South Asian Concern: PO Box 43, Sutton, Surrey SM2 5WL Tel: 0181-770-9717.

Other Organisations

NATECLA (National Association for Teaching English and Other Community Languages to Adults): National Centre, South Birmingham College, 524 Stratford Road, Birmingham B11 4AJ Tel: 0121-694-5070.

Office for National Statistics: 1 Drummond Gate, Pimlico, London SW1V 2QQ Tel: 0171-242-0262 ext 2208 or 2243.

The Asian Family Counselling Service: Offers marriage guidance and other counselling support, both over the phone and one-to-one (London-based) Tel: 0181-997-5749.

The Commission for Racial Equality, Elliot House, 10-12 Allington Street, London SW1 Tel: 0171-828-7022.

The Refugee Council (The Refugee Advisers Support Unit): 3 Bondway, London SW8 1SJ Tel: 0171-820-3000 or 0171-582-6922 Fax 0171-582-9929.